THE
Photographer's
MANUAL

THE Photographer's MANUAL

How to get the best picture every time, with any kind of camera

JOHN FREEMAN

HH
HERMES
HOUSE

DEDICATION
FOR MY MOTHER
AND IN MEMORY
OF MY FATHER

THANKS TO
LEEDS PHOTOVISUAL LIMITED
NIKON UK LIMITED
PUSH ONE LIMITED
THE STUDIO WORKSHOP LIMITED
TAPESTRY LIMITED
MORTIMER AND RHONA AT MANIQUE MODELS
MEL FOR HER MAKE-UP SKILLS

ACKNOWLEDGEMENTS

This book would not have been possible without the help and support of numerous friends, colleagues and organizations. In particular I would like to thank Joanna Lorenz, who saw it as a good idea, and Penelope Cream, my editor, who made it all happen, sometimes in circumstances when it appeared it might not! Also, Mike Morey for his design skills, my assistants Alex Freeman, Octavia Hedley-Dent, Kate Freeman, Luke Freeman, Sue Sharpe and a special thank you to Vanessa Ephson for being there.

Many thanks also to Isabelle Blondiau, Paul Cochrane, Stuart Davies, Jack Dooley, Melanie Ephson, Teresa Freeman, Roe Freeman, Frome Photo Centre, Samuel Greenhill, Sandra Hadfield, Lisa Haleran, Ami Hanson, George Heap, Dom Linell, John Mair, Yvonne and Luz Mosquera, Lorenzo Nardo, Theresa Neenan, Tarjit, Gurmeet and Jaspreet Parmar, Megan and Briony Plant, Denise and Lizzie Reynolds, Rikki Sarah, Meg, Jessica and Emma Simmonds, Jen Sherrin, Laila Walker, the Wapping Playgroup, Charlie Whiteside, Patrick and Rainbow Wiseman, David White and Carol Yun.

All photographs by John Freeman.

The photograph of the Palace of Holyroodhouse is reproduced by gracious permission of Her Majesty Queen Elizabeth II.

The illustrations for the video still camera and photocopying sections by Al Morrison.

This edition published by Hermes House
27 West 20th Street, New York, NY 10011

HERMES HOUSE books are available for bulk purchase for sales promotion and for premium use. For details, write or call the sales director, Hermes House, 27 West 20th Street, New York, NY 10011; (800) 354-9657

ISBN 1-84038-430-1

Publisher Joanna Lorenz
Project Editor Penelope Cream
Designer Michael Morey
Illustrator John Hutchinson
Cover design Caroline Grimshaw

Also published as *Practical Photography*

Printed and bound in Hong Kong

© Anness Publishing Limited 1993, 1999

Photographs © John Freeman

1 3 5 7 9 10 8 6 4 2

CONTENTS

Getting Started

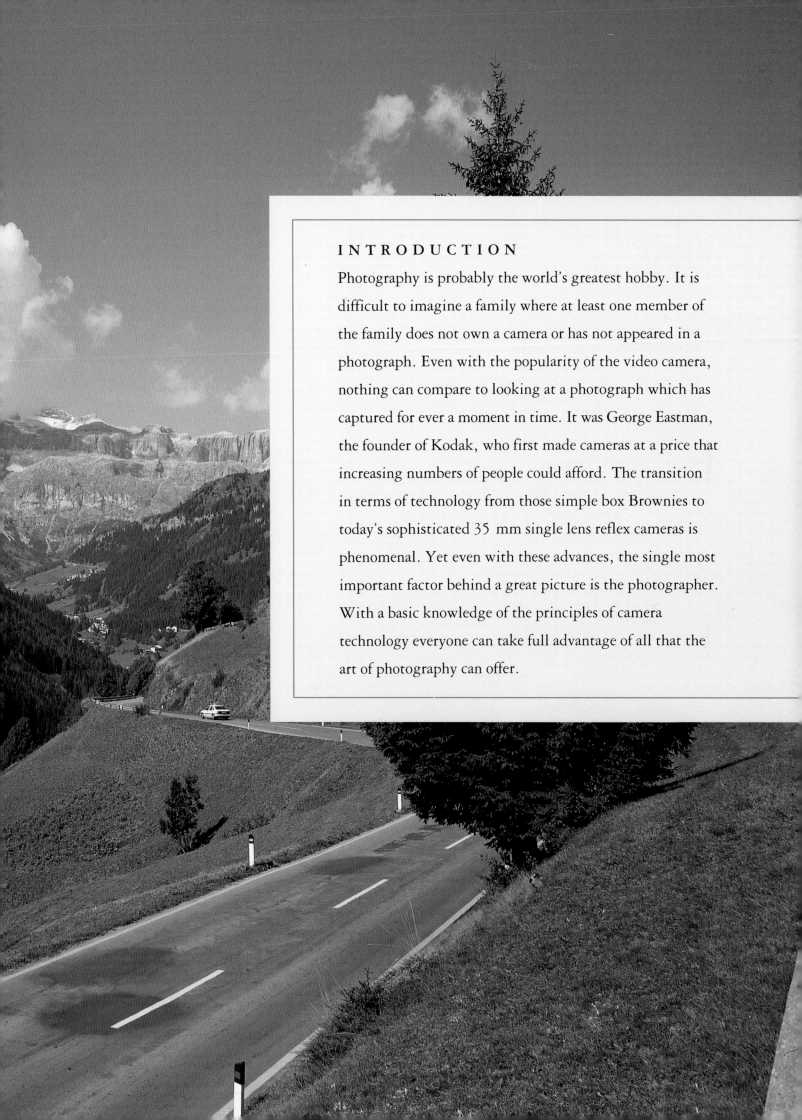

INTRODUCTION

Photography is probably the world's greatest hobby. It is difficult to imagine a family where at least one member of the family does not own a camera or has not appeared in a photograph. Even with the popularity of the video camera, nothing can compare to looking at a photograph which has captured for ever a moment in time. It was George Eastman, the founder of Kodak, who first made cameras at a price that increasing numbers of people could afford. The transition in terms of technology from those simple box Brownies to today's sophisticated 35 mm single lens reflex cameras is phenomenal. Yet even with these advances, the single most important factor behind a great picture is the photographer. With a basic knowledge of the principles of camera technology everyone can take full advantage of all that the art of photography can offer.

The question that professional photographers are probably asked most frequently is, 'What is the best camera I can buy?' Unfortunately there is no simple answer. Even though many people consider the Rolls-Royce to be the best motor car in the world, it is not suited to all uses: it would be at a distinct disadvantage in a Formula One race. In the same way, there are some cameras that some photographers consider the 'Rolls-Royce' of their kind yet it does not always follow that these are the best choice for all shooting situations. Undoubtedly the camera that has proved most popular is the 35 mm SLR.

The important aspects to consider when choosing a camera are application, variety of accessories and cost. The range of cameras available is wide, yet each type is very distinct in its uses. Photographers should examine the different models and decide which might be the most suitable for their requirements. Ultimately, however, whichever camera is used, the elements that go to make up the final image will be those that the photographer brings to the camera, rather than the number of dials or knobs it has. Even a disposable camera can produce a good picture in the hands of an attentive and enthusiastic photographer who takes care with composition, gives thought to foreground and background, and notes the prevailing lighting conditions. Great shots can be achieved with even the most modest budget and a little technical knowledge.

The more money the photographer is prepared to spend, the more sophisticated the camera can be; usually the different models will include autoexposure and built-in flash (although this may not always be very powerful), motor drive, zoom lens, autofocus, and automatic rewinding of the film back into the cassette when the reel is complete. Models at the cheaper end of the range have a fixed lens and focus limit so that bright daylight conditions are required. The more expensive models obviously expand the creative possibilities of the 35 mm camera, although even the basic models are reliable and will produce effective shots.

THE 35 MM CAMERA

The compact 35 mm camera (so-called because it uses 35 mm film) is an ideal

• The range of 35 mm cameras is enormous, from a disposable model, BOTTOM LEFT, through to the most sophisticated autometering and autofocusing types, FAR RIGHT.

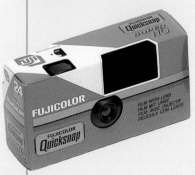

model for those beginning photography or those who want a simple all-in-one with the minimum of accessories and adjustments. There is a vast range of different models within the 35 mm category. The simplest, and cheapest, will be a 'point-and-shoot' version without a built-in exposure meter or flash where the film is loaded and advanced manually.

THE SINGLE REFLEX (SLR) CAMERA

This camera is portable and extremely adaptable. Since its introduction approximately 50 years ago, the SLR (single lens reflex) has proved to be one of the most popular cameras available. The original design has now evolved

into a multiplicity of models, the majority of which have a formidable array of lenses and accessories.

When you look through the viewfinder of an SLR camera what you see is what the lens 'sees'. This is because there is a mirror behind the lens that reflects the image up to a device called a pentaprism. This turns the image the right way up and the correct way round, and is situated on the top of the camera in front of the viewfinder. In normal conditions, when the shutter release button is pressed several functions operate in a fraction of a second. First the mirror flips up 45

degrees so that light can pass through the lens onto the film. The aperture you have chosen stops down. The focal plane shutter opens for the amount of time you have chosen on the shutter speed dial and then closes, then the aperture opens up to its full extent and the mirror comes back down so that you can view the scene again.

Using readily available 35 mm film, the basic SLR model can be adapted by the addition of all sorts of equipment, including telephoto or zoom lenses, motor drive and flash units. This means that it is the ideal 'system' camera; it can be adapted as quickly or as slowly as budget allows. An extra advantage to

the SLR is that the top-of-the-range models and accessories popular with professional photographers can be hired at specialist camera shops. In this way, a vast amount of equipment is available for minimum financial outlay.

THE RANGEFINDER CAMERA

This is another model of camera which has proved very popular with professional photographers. The most famous brand of rangefinder is the Leica; the French photojournalist Henri Cartier-Bresson shot nearly all his most memorable pictures using one.

In contrast to the SLR camera, the rangefinder allows the subject to be seen through a separate viewfinder rather than through the lens. In the centre of the viewfinder are two images. When the lens is focused on the subject these two images become aligned with one another and the picture will then be sharp. This method of working is preferred by some photographers who find that the camera is quieter to operate and is less prone to being affected by vibration as there is no mirror to flip up. Although the rangefinder does not have quite as wide

a range of accessories as the SLR, it is a sturdy and reliable camera with extremely high-quality lenses. The rangefinder is available in 35 mm or medium format models.

THE SLR MEDIUM FORMAT CAMERA

These cameras come between the 35 mm and the large format cameras in size and application. They take pictures in a variety of formats including 6 × 4.5 cm, 6 × 6 cm and 6 × 7 cm. These cameras have extensive ranges of lenses and accessories and are much favoured by professional photographers. They are much bulkier than 35 mm cameras and are usually used on a tripod, although they can be hand-held. They are the only cameras that use 120 or 220 ISO film, available in roll or cassette form.

THE 5 × 4 CAMERA

This is a large format, tripod-mounted camera which takes photographs where the transparencies or negatives are 5 × 4 in (12.5 × 10 cm). The film is loaded into dark slides, each one holding just two sheets. There is no viewfinder in the conventional sense: the image is seen upside-down and back-to-front on a ground glass screen. In order to see the image and keep out any stray light the photographer covers the camera and his head with a dark cloth. Despite the rather old-fashioned appearance of the camera, many models are in fact brand-new, extremely sophisticated and can be very expensive.

The range of applications of the 5 × 4 camera is very varied both in the studio and on location. It produces pictures with excellent clarity and sharpness of detail. However, it would

● Medium format and large format cameras, such as the 5 × 4 in, FAR RIGHT, are generally favoured by professionals.

not be the best choice for spontaneous or action shots where a more portable camera with speedy shooting capability might be more suitable.

THE INSTANT AND POLAROID CAMERA

Instant picture cameras such as the Polaroid offer another dimension to picture-taking. After the picture is taken, the film is impregnated with the chemicals required for processing the image and the picture begins to appear only seconds after the shutter is pressed; development is complete within minutes. As well as providing an immediate image of the subject, these cameras also offer as many possibilities for creative photography as their conventional counterparts. Many professional photographers attach special Polaroid backs to their standard cameras; once they have composed the image and calculated the exposure they will take a Polaroid picture to ensure everything is perfect before shooting on conventional film. Polaroid backs are available for all cameras from 35 mm size to 10 × 8 models.

THE VIDEO STILL CAMERA

The video still camera is a relatively new type of camera; it uses a computer disk instead of conventional film and the pictures can be viewed on a television screen or video monitor, or sent away to be made into prints. Although still in its early stages, this form of photography could change the nature of picture-taking in the future.

EQUIPMENT: LENSES

Just as there is no one camera that is ideal for every shooting situation, the same is true of lenses. Some lenses in certain situations have distinct advantages over others. An extra element of challenge can be added to photography by experimentation with different lenses, perhaps applying a particular lens to a situation in which it is not normally used.

LENSES FOR 35 MM SLR CAMERAS

Most 35 mm SLR cameras are purchased with what is known as a 'standard' lens. This has a focal length of about 50 mm and will give an angle of view roughly equivalent to what we see with our own eyes. Its maximum aperture in the region of f1.8, but faster lenses such as f1.4 and f1.2 are

available. At a later date one of these faster lenses could prove useful.

LENS MOUNTS

All SLR cameras have interchangeable lenses, attached to the camera by means of a mount. There are several different sorts of mount, the most popular being the bayonet mount. This is operated by depressing or sliding a small button positioned on the camera body near the

lens. The lens can then be turned 45 degrees in a clockwise direction and pulled gently forward from the camera body, and another lens inserted using the reverse procedure.

CHOICE OF LENSES

Interchangeability of lenses opens up a

● A selection of zoom and telephoto lenses.

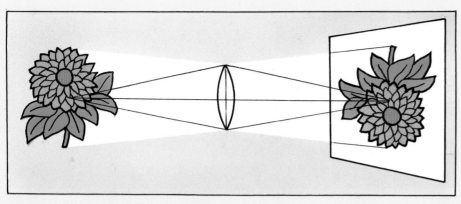

● ABOVE The subject is reproduced through a lens upside-down on the film.

vast array of options and is probably the biggest single factor in improving photographic creativity. Having chosen a camera and standard lens, it is advisable to consider purchasing two other lenses at the same time or very shortly after. These would probably be a wide angle lens in the focal range of 28–35 mm, and a telephoto lens in the 85–135 mm range.

WIDE ANGLE LENSES

A wide angle lens gives a wider angle of view, so more of the area in front of the camera will appear in the shot. Like any piece of equipment there are disadvantages as well as benefits; the

● Wide angle and medium telephoto lenses.

most common in the case of the wide angle lens occurs in landscape photography where the foreground may lack interest so the eye is not naturally led to the central point of the picture.

On the other hand, a wide angle lens allows subjects to be photographed much closer to the lens than usual, while at the same time keeping the background in focus. In some cases this effect can greatly enhance a composition.

TELEPHOTO LENSES

A medium telephoto lens has many advantages. As well as bringing distant objects closer, it is a superb lens for portraits. It has definite advantages over a wide angle lens in this situation as, when used straight onto someone's face, a wide angle lens will add an unflattering, albeit at times amusing, bulbous quality. A telephoto lens in the region of 100 mm enables the photographer to stand some distance away, making the subject more relaxed and allowing an unblocked light source. The lens will very slightly compress the image, making for a far more pleasing portrait. The depth of field will be less, so the background can be put out of focus and a part of the subject's face, such as the eyes, can be highlighted.

ZOOM LENSES

Many photographers find these lenses very convenient; they give the benefit of being adjustable to an infinite variety of focal lengths which can make composition of pictures much easier. Although in a technical sense a zoom lens will not produce the same quality as a prime lens of a given focal length, under most conditions the difference will be apparent only to an eagle eye.

Depending on the type of photography that is of interest, wide angle and telephoto lenses that are of a very extreme range have limited applications and can easily be under-used; their purchase should therefore be considered very seriously.

FISHEYE LENSES

A fisheye lens can be used to dramatic effect, but as an everyday piece of equipment it has limited applications and its novelty value can quickly wear off.

● Ultra-telephoto lenses.

A MACRO LENS

The macro lens allows the photographer to get very close to the subject without the need for special close-up attachments. Depending on the lens used, small objects can be magnified to produce a final print which shows them life-size. Many of the lenses mentioned here in the 28–300 mm range have this facility built in and it is often worth considering paying a bit extra at the outset if this is of interest.

SHIFT OR PERSPECTIVE CONTROL LENS

The shift or perspective control lens allows photography of a subject that is very tall, without the problem of converging verticals; this occurs when the sides of the subject taper toward the top of the picture. The conventional rule for preventing this from happening is to ensure that the film plane is parallel to the vertical plane of the subject and then all vertical lines will remain straight in the final shot. However, with a fixed lens the top of a very tall subject is usually cut off, but with a shift lens the axis can be altered, allowing the camera to remain straight while the lens is moved upwards: the top of the building will then come into view.

● Fisheye, ultra-wide angle and macro lenses.

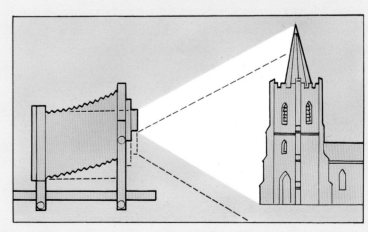

● BELOW By using a shift, or perspective control, lens, as opposed to moving the camera, subjects such as tall buildings can be perfectly framed.

ACCESSORIES

There are many accessories that can be added to a basic camera unit when building up a comprehensive 'system'. It is important to bear in mind that no accessory on its own is going to provide a magic formula for improving photographic skills. Accessories lend technical help, yet it is the photographer's eye for seeing a good picture that is the essence of photography.

A UV FILTER

Having decided on and purchased the camera, the next thing to buy is an UV filter. This can be kept on the lens at all times, whether you are using colour or black and white film. As well as reducing the amount of ultraviolet light passing through the lens (cutting down haze and minimizing the risk of a blue cast appearing on the film), it will also protect the lens itself. It is much cheaper to replace even a good quality glass filter if it gets scratched than a scratched lens. Consider buying a UV filter for each lens.

As well as the UV filter, there is a whole selection of special filters and holders available. These range from colour correction and colour-balancing filters to special effect filters and masks.

THE LENS HOOD

This should be bought at the same time as the camera. Look at any picture of professional photographers at work and they will all be using lens hoods. The hood prevents most stray light from entering the lens. Stray light causes flare and can ruin the picture. It may be caused by sunlight falling directly into the lens or being reflected off a building or shiny surface. If you are in any doubt as to the necessity of a lens hood, next time you are walking or driving into the sun, notice how you need to shield your eyes from the light with a hand or

the sun visor in the car. A lens hood works in exactly the same way for the camera lens.

A TRIPOD

A tripod keeps the camera steady during shooting at long exposures. To be effective the tripod must be rigid. Some tripods are very flimsy when fully extended so it is often well worth paying a little extra money for a truly sturdy model. Tripods are

available in many sizes from the smallest, which are about 15 cm (6 in) high, to much larger, heavy-duty models which can extend to well over 3 m (10 ft).

Some tripods come complete with all attachments; others need a head, the part that fixes the camera to the tripod. Heads can vary and it is important to look at several before making a final choice. The most common type is the 'pan and tilt' head which allows the

● A combination of accessories aids the able photographer to enhance shots, and to be more versatile in a variety of situations.

adjusted to different heights. Obviously, a monopod will not stand unaided but it can be used to help brace the camera. Professional photographers at a football match, for example, nearly always use a monopod.

A CABLE RELEASE

A cable release can be attached to any camera which allows it to be screwed into the shutter release button; when the plunger on the end of the cable is depressed it fires the shutter without the need for any direct manual contact. It is often used in conjunction with a tripod when shooting at slow speeds to reduce the vibration that often occurs when the shutter is released manually.

Some cable releases are now available for SLR cameras. When the cable is depressed half-way the mirror-up mechanism is activated. Any vibration that occurs when the mirror goes up is then eliminated by this intermediate stage in the shutter release process. When the cable plunger is depressed fully the shutter is fired and the camera remains steady.

A CARRYING CASE

A case to carry all the accessories is convenient and also provides protection for equipment. The most effective cases have hard outer shells, and compartments moulded from foam rubber to hold the individual accessories. Soft cases are also available but these may not be suitable for very delicate items. Many cases are obviously meant for carrying cameras; this attracts thieves, so do lock them out of sight if left in a car. Insuring expensive photographic equipment is becoming increasingly costly; if you think that you may have to leave equipment in a locked vehicle, make sure that the insurance policy covers theft from cars.

camera to be moved smoothly through 360 degrees – the 'pan' movement. At the same time it can be adjusted vertically; this is usually in the range of 90 degrees forwards and 45 degrees backwards – this is the 'tilt' movement. (If an angle of 45 degrees is not sufficient, turn the camera round and use the head back-to-front.)

Another useful head is the 'ball and socket' version. Normally this has two knobs that allow the camera to be

moved when fixed to the tripod in much the same direction as the pan and tilt head, yet is far less cumbersome.

A MONOPOD

Since many tripods are often bulky, some places such as churches, buildings of historical interest and museums do not allow their use without a permit. One solution to this may be to use a monopod. As its name suggests, it consists of a single leg which can be

ACCESSORIES (continued)

Flash guns

Ring flash

FLASH ATTACHMENTS

Most SLR cameras do not have built-in flash so it is certainly worth purchasing a flash unit to attach to the 'hot shoe' or accessory shoe on the camera. Some are quite compact but are nevertheless sophisticated and powerful.

The more powerful flash units are mounted on a bracket that is screwed into the base plate of the camera, and linked to the flash synchronization socket on the camera by means of a cable. When the shutter is activated a signal is sent to fire the flash.

EXPOSURE METERS

Although most cameras now have some sort of built-in mechanism for evaluating exposure, a separate hand-held exposure meter is very useful. Basic photoelectric meters need no batteries and register the amount of light available. Although reliable, they are not as powerful nor as sensitive as the battery-powered meters; many of these can be used as flash meters as well as for reading ambient light.

Bellows

Flash and ambient
light meter

Set of extension rings

Battery-powered
exposure meter

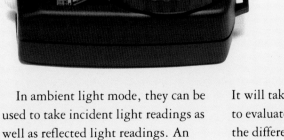

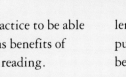

Photoelectric meter

In ambient light mode, they can be used to take incident light readings as well as reflected light readings. An incident light reading is taken when the meter is placed on or near the subject and pointed towards the light source to take a reading. A reflected light reading is taken when the meter is directed at the subject from the camera position.

It will take a little practice to be able to evaluate the various benefits of the different types of reading.

EXTENSION RINGS
OR BELLOWS

These are used in conjunction with SLR cameras and allow close-up photography of detail in stunning clarity. Close-up

lenses can be used for the same purpose but extension rings give a far better result.

The rings or bellows are attached to the body of the camera on the lens mounting; the lens is then attached to the front of these. The rings offer a single magnification whereas with the bellows the magnification is variable.

CARE OF EQUIPMENT

GETTING STARTED

Cameras and lenses are delicate and expensive instruments that need to be treated with care. Water, dust, dirt and grit are the worst enemies, although leaving a camera in bright sunlight or in the glove compartment of a car will not do it any good either, and so any strong heat should be avoided. If the camera is taken to a sandy beach, keep it wrapped in a plastic bag when not in use. Even on the calmest days sand seems to get into every crack; extra care needs to be taken as sand can easily ruin expensive equipment.

When a camera is not in use it should be kept in its case or together with the other pieces of equipment in a proper camera case. If it is not going to be used for some time the batteries should be removed; if left in the camera they may corrode the contacts and cause irreparable damage.

LENSES AND FILTERS

Always keep a skylight UV filter on the lenses. This will keep out UV light and will help protect the lenses themselves. This filter can be kept on the lenses permanently, with either colour or black and white film. A scratched filter is cheaper to replace than a damaged lens. If the filter or lens becomes dirty first blow away the dust and any other particles of dirt. The most efficient way of doing this is to use a pressurized can of air. Many of these products are ozone-friendly and do not contain CFC propellants. Alternatively, use a soft brush with a blower attached to it. If neither of these pieces of equipment is available, simply blow gently onto the surface. The next stage is to remove any grease by gently wiping the lens or filter with a soft lens tissue or lens cloth.

If something jams in or on the camera and the fault is not apparent never force the piece, as more serious damage could be caused. If the lens or camera develops a serious fault send it

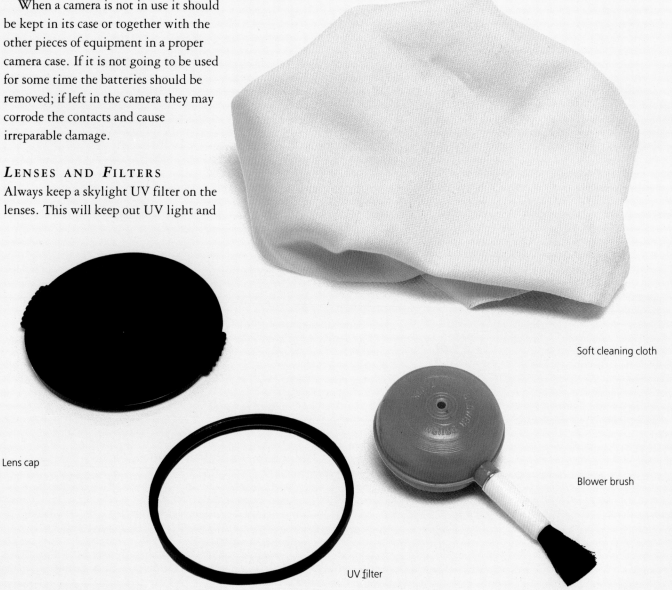

Soft cleaning cloth

Lens cap

Blower brush

UV filter

to a reputable camera repair shop. If it is still under guarantee, return it to the dealer or direct to the manufacturer.

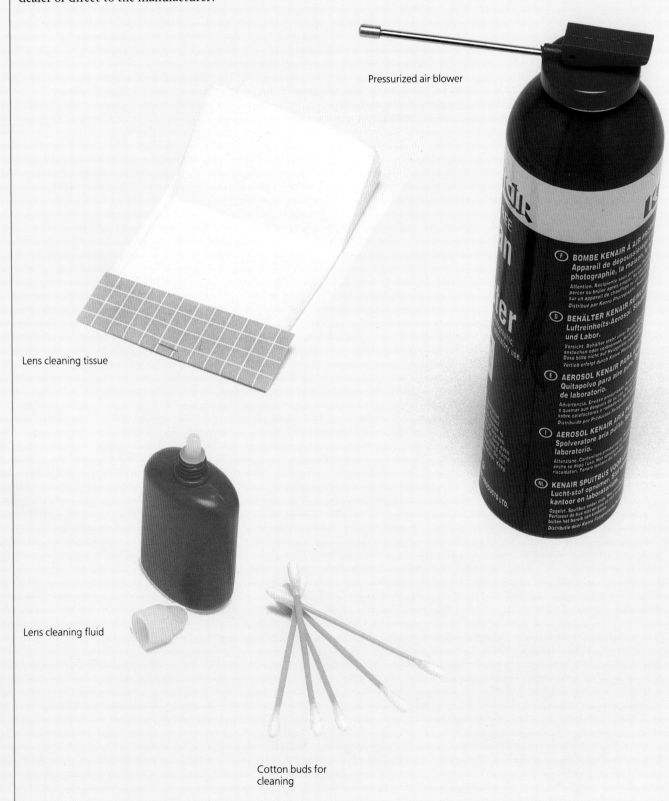

Pressurized air blower

Lens cleaning tissue

Lens cleaning fluid

Cotton buds for cleaning

Negatives and transparencies form an archive of images, preserving memories and moments forever. A visual diary of children can be built up from birth. These children may well have children of their own, and even grandchildren. What better way of seeing a family's development, a history of its background, even the country it has come from, than in a series of photographs? If all the negatives have been kept in good condition, then future generations can assemble a fascinating visual family tree.

It is only too easy to mislay colour negatives and transparencies. This can be a great pity; if prints are destroyed, or friends or relatives would like copies of pictures, others can always be produced from the negatives. While it is possible to reproduce an image from an existing print the quality will not be as good.

STORAGE OF NEGATIVES

Negatives are returned with prints in a wallet. If they are dated and catalogued properly these provide a perfectly adequate storage system. The wallets can be filed in a drawer with a simple log of what they are. Alternatively, special negative storage filing systems are available; these consist of double-thickness plastic or paper sheets with pockets or channels for holding the transparencies. The sheets are then stored in binders or hung from metal rods in filing cabinet drawers.

STORAGE OF TRANSPARENCIES

If they are mounted as slides, transparencies can be stored in slide boxes, grooved to take a mounted slide, with an index for cataloguing the pictures. If the slides are for projection, they can be kept in a slide projector magazine or tray. These have dust covers and can be indexed as before.

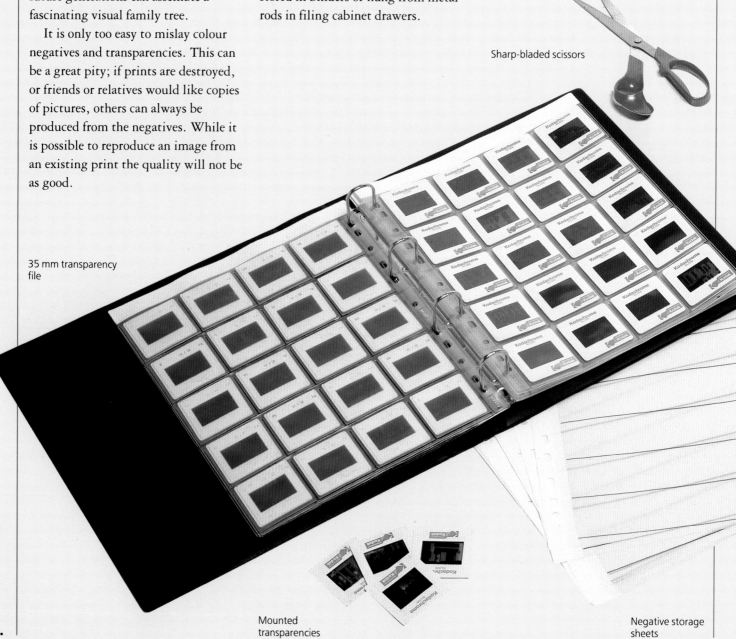

Sharp-bladed scissors

35 mm transparency file

Mounted transparencies

Negative storage sheets

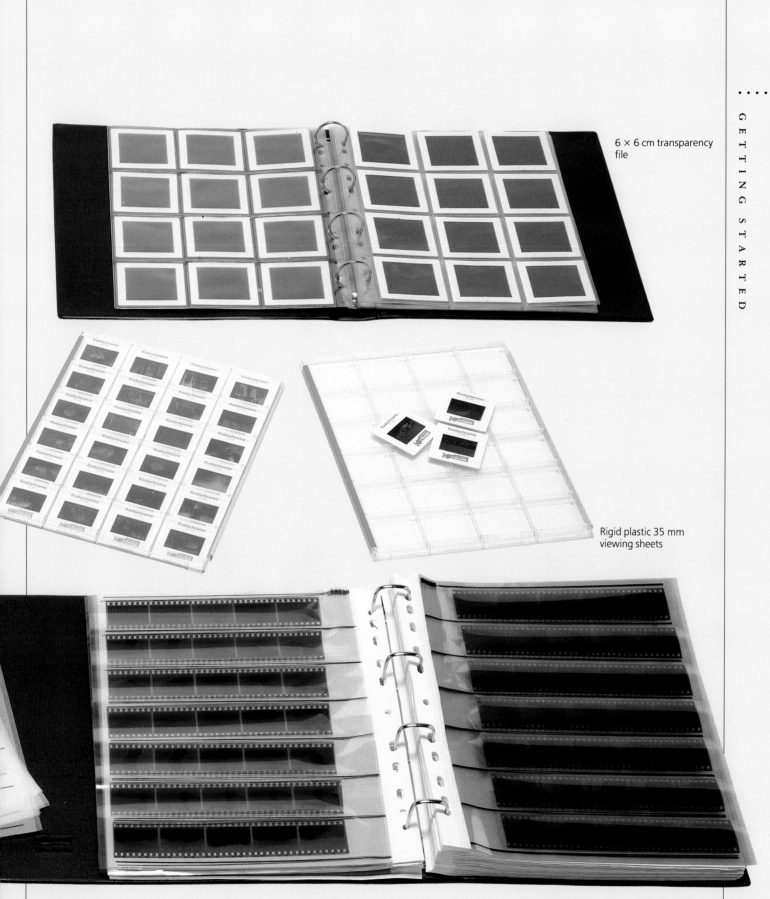

6 × 6 cm transparency file

Rigid plastic 35 mm viewing sheets

Negative storage file

There are two main types of colour film used.

• Colour reversal film produces transparencies that can be mounted as slides and projected or viewed with a slide viewer or on a light box. Transparencies can also be made into prints, either directly, or from what is called an internegative, which involves photographing the transparency onto the other kind of film, colour negative film.

• Colour negative film is the type used to make prints.

Most professional photographers use colour reversal film, whereas most amateurs prefer colour negative.

Both types of film come in a full range of sizes, from the small 110 up through 35 mm to 10 × 8 in (30 × 20 cm) sheet film. They also come in various speeds. These are given as an ISO (International Standards Organization) number from about 25 for the slowest up to 1600 and beyond for the fastest. The slower the film, the finer the grain and sharpness, and the greater the colour saturation and contrast. 1600 ISO film can be uprated to 3200 ISO and more for work in low light but the result will be very grainy – an effect which may be sought deliberately.

UPRATING FILM AND DX CODING

Uprating, also called speed readjustment, means using film as if it had a higher ISO rating than it actually does, and so shortening exposure time. Uprated film needs a longer development time, and if you uprate any film you must let the laboratory know that you have done this so that they can 'push', or extend, development. Some laboratories charge extra for handling uprated film. Generally only colour reversal film is uprated since the processing for all colour negative films is the same. However, a few colour negative films are now made in such a way that they can be uprated.

35 mm film is now DX coded: this means that the film cassette has a bar code on it. Nearly all new cameras have tiny sensors that read the code and automatically change the camera's ISO setting to the appropriate speed. If you

want to uprate the film you should buy bar code override stickers to put on the cassette. Alternatively, if your camera has an exposure compensating dial, you can adjust this to uprate the film. In either case you must inform the laboratory of what you have done.

LIGHTING

There are two types of colour reversal film: one for daylight and electronic flash, the other for tungsten light (ordinary lamps). If daylight film is used in tungsten light the shots will come out very warm, with an orange and red glow to them. If tungsten-balanced film is used in daylight the pictures will have a blue cast. Although both these films are made for the specified lighting

conditions there is no reason why they should not be used in different lighting to create a special effect. Either of them can also be used with a light-balancing filter. Using an 85B filter, which looks orange, on a camera allows tungsten film to be used in daylight or with electronic flash to get a normal colour balance. An 80B filter, which is bluish, allows daylight film to be used in tungsten film with normal results.

Until recently there was only one kind of colour negative film which was used in both daylight and tungsten light. Any colour cast was corrected at the printing stage. However, there are now several colour negative films available that are made specifically for use in tungsten light.

ACCURATE EXPOSURE

Exposure needs to be far more accurate for colour reversal film than for colour negative because the transparency is the final result. With colour negative film any inaccuracies in the negative can be corrected at the print stage. Where accuracy is required it is a great help to make a test with an instant film such as Polaroid so that any adjustments can be made on the spot.

INFRARED FILM

You might also like to experiment with infrared film. This gives unusual though unpredictable results, quite different from the colours we normally see. For example, foliage becomes magenta and pale skin tones green.

FILM TYPES: *2*

Over the last two decades shooting in colour has become the norm in photography, and amateurs have almost abandoned black and white. This is a great pity, for many colour photographs would look better in monochrome. Some of today's best known photographers, such as Steven Miesels, Herb Ritts and the late Robert Mapplethorpe, are famous for their work in black and white, and exhibitions and books of their work consist almost entirely of black and white prints.

Undoubtedly most people relate immediately to a colour photograph, which is hardly surprising as we see the world in colour. Therefore any colour image is relatively acceptable, while an image in black and white has to be spot on for it to get the attention it deserves. Another reason for the neglect of black and white is that the film is now almost as expensive to buy and more expensive to process than colour. It also takes longer to process: you cannot get your prints back in an hour!

Unlike colour film, which has negative and reversal types, black and white film is almost always negative. There is no need to worry about colour balance, as black and white film can be used under any lighting conditions. It comes in speeds from very slow, such as 25 ISO, to ultra-fast at 3200 ISO – and even this can be 'push processed' to increase the speed still further. Slow film gives very fine grain and good shadow detail, and pictures can be enlarged with little loss of quality. In contrast the faster films are generally very grainy and the shadow detail inferior.

BLACK AND WHITE FILM

When black and white film is processed it is usual to make a contact sheet. This means that, for instance, a 36 exposure roll of film is cut into six strips of six negatives. These are placed on a 10 × 8 in (30 × 20 cm) sheet of printing paper to make a positive print. On this contact sheet you select and mark the negatives you want to have made into enlarged prints. In making this selection you can ask for unwanted parts

of the negative to be cropped out — draw the area you want on the contact sheet as a guide. You can also ask the printer to angle the masking frame, which holds the printing paper in place on the enlarger, to tilt the picture. This can often improve the overall composition. Some laboratories can produce enlarged 'contacts' which give a better idea of how enlargements will look. The whole film is printed on a 16 × 12 in (40 × 30 cm), 20 × 16 in (50 × 30 cm) or 24 × 20 in (60 × 50 cm) sheet.

Prints can be ordered in different finishes, from matt to glossy. Paper types include resin-coated, which has a plastic surface that gives faster development, needs less washing and dries faster than the traditional type. The older fibre-based paper, which gives a more subtle effect, is favoured by photographers for exhibitions and portfolios. On both these papers you can have toned prints. Sepia is the best known tone, but there are others. Some are more suitable for fibre-based paper, others for resin-coated. You can also hand colour your prints. This old technique is now enjoying a revival. It calls for special colouring media.

SPECIAL BLACK AND WHITE FILM

Black and white slides for projection are made on special 'positive' black and white film. There is also black and white instant film, made by Polaroid. Infrared black and white film gives unusual results: pictures taken in daylight look like night scenes. This film should be tested before you use it in earnest, to avoid unexpected results.

FILTERS FOR BLACK AND WHITE

Although you do not need to use light balancing filters for black and white film, some coloured filters can add interest to your images. For example, a yellow filter will darken a blue sky and make the clouds stand out sharply. A red filter will exaggerate the effect: even a blue sky with white clouds will look positively stormy.

THE HUMAN EYE AND THE CAMERA

We see the world in colour, so it is hardly surprising that most people tend to load their cameras with colour film. Even before the invention of colour film black and white prints were toned or sometimes hand coloured to add realism.

Technical improvements in colour film have made it possible for everyone to get a reasonably exposed photograph. But exposure is not the only element of a successful colour image. In the same way as a painter controls the colours on his palette, the way we combine colours in photographs, and juxtapose different and complementary hues, plays a vital role in achieving a successful image.

THE HUMAN EYE AND FILM

The colours we see are reflected off the objects we look at. The light that falls on these objects constantly changes, and with it their colours. Daylight is warmer – that is, redder – at the beginning and end of the day than at midday. Weather also changes the quality of daylight. On an overcast day we see colour as cooler – bluer – than in bright sunshine. Hazy sunlight gives muted colours. However, the most important element in colour vision is not the eye but the brain. If we know that a jacket is a particular shade of red we will see that shade of red at any time of day, in any weather, and even indoors under artificial light – ordinary tungsten bulbs throw out a light strongly biased towards the orange and red end of the spectrum, and give colours markedly different from those produced by sunlight.

Film reacts differently. When we move indoors from daylight our vision adjusts to the change in light quality. But if we load a camera with a film made for use in daylight, and use it to photograph the red jacket first out of doors then indoors under tungsten light, the first shot will look about right but the second shot will have a strong orange cast to it. If we use film balanced for tungsten light, the indoor shot will look fine but the outdoor one will be skewed towards the other end of the spectrum, with a blue-violet cast.

It is important to understand how our eyes record colour, and how colour film does it, and to experiment with these effects, in order to create successful colour photographs.

● The juxtaposition of varied coloured images produces a startlingly vibrant collage of contrasting and complementary shades and tones.

SEEING IN BLACK AND WHITE

Taking photographs in black and white is a most rewarding exercise. It is sad that most people today would not dream of putting anything other than colour film in their cameras. Undoubtedly this is because they want their photographs to record the way they remember a particular scene. Yet the absence of colour in a black and white photograph can make a far more striking interpretation of that scene. And since black and white imagery is an interpretation rather than a mere record, the onus is on the photographer to create a picture through the use of texture and tone; these are important considerations in colour photography, but in black and white they are paramount.

If you have two cameras, try loading one with black and white and the other with colour. When you compare your prints you might be surprised at the power of the black and white images.

TONAL RANGE

The tonal range from black through various shades of grey to white is known as the grey scale. Professional photographic stores sell charts of these scales called step wedges, which can be used to analyse a photograph. A black and white print where most of the tones are from the extremes of the scale —without any mid-tones — is referred to as a high-contrast print. If these tones are mostly towards the white end it is called a high-key picture. A picture where most of the tones are near the black end is a low-key print. One that uses the full range of tones is called a full-tone print.

One of the great exponents of black and white photography was the American Ansel Adams. His landscapes combine stunning composition with a powerful grasp of tonal range. They are worth studying.

● ABOVE This picture emphasizes the soft, velvety appearance of the girl's skin. She is lit using a single studio flash unit fitted with a large diffuser or soft box. As its name suggests, this gives a very soft and even light. The picture was shot on the same film, 100 ISO, as was used for the image of the older man.

● LEFT By shooting this ship-building dock threatened with closure in black and white, the mood is emphasized much more than it would be in colour. The print was deliberately made darker to reinforce this image of despair.

● LEFT This studio picture shows a good tonal range. The black at the extreme end of the scale is rich and even, and the mid-tones show a well-defined gradation. The lines and wrinkles of the man's skin are enhanced by the use of black and white. One main light was used to the right with a fill-in light on the other side. A light above the head was used to illuminate the hair. The shot was taken on 100 ISO film.

● BELOW If you are in doubt as to whether a shot should be in colour or black and white and you have two cameras, shoot both as here. The black and white print was deliberately printed on a hard paper to bring out the contrast in the grass. Both shots were taken with the same wide angle lens within minutes of each other.

PROCESSING YOUR FILM

Once you have taken your photographs you will want to see the results as soon as possible. Many places now offer film processing and claim that they give a unique and professional service; but in fact often the film is collected and sent to a central processing laboratory. Here each film is given a computer identification code and they are all joined together in one huge reel like a movie film. The films are processed and printed in rapid succession, the prints cut up and put in wallets, and back everything goes to the shop where you handed in the film.

This sort of processing does not produce results of very good quality, nor is it consistent. If you send the same negative to be printed at the same laboratory several times, the chances are that each time it will come back with a different colour cast. In order to obtain the best results with expensive equipment, or when you have taken the greatest care in composing and exposing your pictures make sure the processing laboratory is a good one.

THE PROFESSIONAL WAY

A professional photographer, especially one who uses colour reversal film, has a close relationship with the technicians at his laboratory. The laboratory will maintain the highest standards, simply because if it does not, photographers will not use it any more.

A professional laboratory can clip test film: before the technicians process the whole film they will cut off the first few frames and process them. You can then check these and ask for adjustments to the rest of the batch. They can adjust the processing in increments of as little as $\frac{1}{8}$ of a stop (one stop is equivalent to the difference between f8 and f11, or between exposure times of $\frac{1}{60}$ and $\frac{1}{125}$ second).

Of course, for this to be worthwhile the film must be consistently exposed, and where the film is cut one or two frames will be lost. There is also a small extra charge for the clip test on top of the cost of processing the rest of the film. Kodachrome Professional film is bought with the processing paid for, but even this can now be clip tested and settings adjusted as necessary.

HOME PROCESSING

The more adventurous can buy home processing kits for both colour negative and colour reversal film, and also for black and white. You do not need to have a fully equipped darkroom to process film. Apart from the equipment in the kit all you need is a processing tank – these come in various sizes, depending on how many films you want to process at once – and a light-tight room or cupboard where you can load the film into the tank. Once this is done, the rest of the process is carried out in normal light, though of course you have to go back into the dark to make prints.

PUSHING AND PULLING

If a film is underexposed, for instance if it is uprated, it needs to be given a longer than normal development time. This is called 'pushing'. Overexposed

● Colour or black and white, transparency or negative – after you have taken your shots, good processing is essential.

film is 'pulled' by being developed for a shorter time than normal. These techniques are common, but they should not be used where they can be avoided because both of them cause a certain loss of picture quality: the harder a film has been pushed or pulled, the greater the loss. There is no substitute for getting your exposures spot on.

ENLARGED PRINTS

Again, a professional laboratory will give you substantially better enlarged prints. You will be able to discuss how you want your picture cropped and

positioned on the masking frame of the enlarger. If a transparency that is to be printed has a colour cast you can ask for this to be corrected. You can even have particular areas of a negative or transparency shaded or printed up to darken or brighten them. This can be important if there is a large discrepancy between the tones in highlighted areas and shadows.

WHAT THE APERTURE DOES

There are different sized apertures on a camera to allow different amounts of light to pass through onto the film. When the shutter is released it allows light to pass through the aperture. It is necessary to have a shutter as well as an aperture because the aperture controls depth of field as well as contributing to the exposure of a film.

The correlation between shutter speed and aperture size is a direct one; the immediate situation or the effect required dictates the necessary combination of shutter speed and size of aperture. If, for instance, an exposure of $\frac{1}{15}$ second and an aperture of f22 are needed, the aperture would get wider as the shutter speed increases

e.g. $\frac{1}{30}$ second   f16
          $\frac{1}{60}$ second   f11
          $\frac{1}{125}$ second   f8

DEPTH OF FIELD

The depth of field is the distance in front of and beyond the sharply focused subject of the picture. With a standard lens set on its widest aperture of f1.8, for example, and a subject 2 yards (1.8 m) from the camera, very little of the background and even less of the foreground would be in focus. However, if the lens is stopped down and the aperture is set to f16 or f22 much more of the background and foreground will be sharp.

With a wide angle lens depth of field will be greater even at wider apertures than it would be with a telephoto lens.

Depth of field plays an important part of the creation of a finished photograph. If, for example, the subject of the picture is a head and shoulders portrait of a person, yet with

a distracting or unattractive background, it can be the depth of field that can be altered to put the background out of focus so that the person is the only clear part of the shot. If, on the other hand, the background is important or the subject is a group of people or objects at different distances from the camera where each one must appear sharp, a small aperture is needed. A small aperture would bring more of the picture into sharp focus.

AUTOMATIC CAMERAS

Some automatic cameras have a system called aperture priority. When the aperture is set the camera automatically adjusts the shutter speed. Care must be taken in cases where the chosen aperture is quite small, e.g. f11 or f16, as the shutter speed selected may be too slow to take an accurate shot without the steadying aid of a tripod or other support.

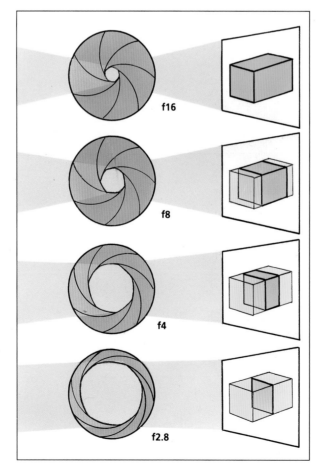

f16

f8

f4

f2.8

● LEFT There is a direct correlation between aperture size and depth of field. As the aperture decreases, more of the subject is in focus.

- This picture was taken using a standard lens at an aperture of f2.8. The girl is in focus and so is the front arm of the seat but everything else is out of focus.

- In this picture a medium telephoto lens was used and focused on the girl. Depth of field is minimal at an aperture of f4.5.

- In this picture an aperture of f8 was used. More of the seat and background are sharper but the distance is still unclear.

- Using the same telephoto lens an aperture of f11 has been used but the background still remains very soft.

- Here the lens was stopped down to f22 and all the seat is sharp and the far distance is only slightly soft. By reducing the size of the aperture more of the picture is brought into focus i.e. the depth of field increases.

- With the lens stopped right down to f32 much more of the picture is in focus, yet it is not as sharp as in the first picture. Depth of field is greater with wide angle lenses than it is with telephoto lenses.

WHAT THE SHUTTER SPEED DOES

● BELOW A leaf shutter (top) and a focal plane shutter (below) in the process of opening.

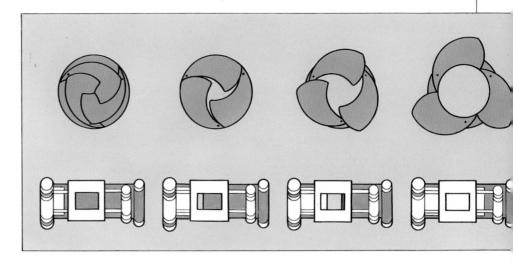

The opening of the shutter of a camera determines the amount of time light is allowed to pass through the lens onto the film. As well as affecting exposure, the shutter speed can also freeze a moving object as a sharp image on film and reduce camera shake.

PORTRAYING FAST-MOVING OBJECTS

For hand-held shots it is virtually impossible to hold the camera completely steady at shutter speeds of $\frac{1}{30}$ second or less without mounting the camera on a tripod or bracing it against a solid support, such as a wall.

Imagine a car or a person passing quickly across a chosen viewpoint. If the shutter speed is set at $\frac{1}{60}$ second or less the moving object would appear blurred on the photograph. However, if the shutter speed were $\frac{1}{250}$ second or more the moving object would be clear, 'frozen' in action. In the case of the car, it can be difficult to tell whether it is moving or stationary; this may result in a dull picture. A better way to illustrate action is to use a slower shutter speed and 'pan' the camera, following the moving object and taking the picture when it is directly in front. This type of photography may take a little practice to perfect but it produces striking images where the background is blurred and the moving object sharp, illustrating very effectively the speed at which it was travelling.

USING FLASH WITH SLR CAMERAS

With SLR cameras the shutter speed should be set to the manufacturers' recommended setting when using flash. This is usually $\frac{1}{60}$ or $\frac{1}{125}$ second. If a faster speed is used, only part of the film will be exposed as the flash will fire before the blinds of the shutter have

● LEFT Shutters at various stages of opening. TOP A leaf shutter. BOTTOM A focal plane shutter.

● BELOW When using flash with a camera that has a focal plane shutter it is important to set the camera at the manufacturer's designated speed. This might be ¹/₁₂₅ second, for instance, or there might be a flash symbol on the shutter speed dial for this. If the speed used is in excess of this setting, only part of the frame will be exposed.

● BELOW LEFT In this picture the camera was mounted on a tripod and a slow shutter speed, ¹/₄ second, was used.

● RIGHT When a long exposure is required, in this case 20 seconds, the shutter was set to the T setting. This meant that when the shutter was fired it remained open until it was depressed again. If the camera only has a setting on the shutter speed dial marked B, the shutter release has to remain depressed.

fully opened. With cameras that have a leaf shutter or a shutter between the lens the flash can be synchronized to any speed. This is a great advantage in situations where flash has to be balanced with daylight.

B AND T SETTINGS

On some shutter speed dials there are two settings marked B and T. When the shutter ring is set to B the shutter will remain open for as long as the shutter release button is depressed. If it is set to T, the shutter will remain open even when the shutter release button is released, closing when the button is depressed again. Both these settings are for use with pictures that require a long exposure.

AUTOMATIC SHUTTER SPEED SELECTION

Some automatic cameras have metering modes called shutter priority. This means that when the shutter speed is adjusted manually the camera selects the aperture automatically.

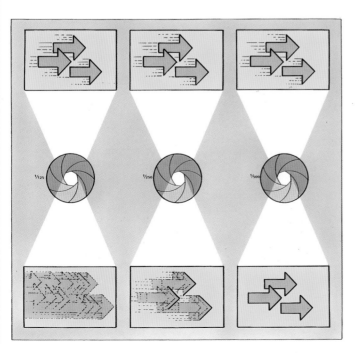

● LEFT If the camera is moved in line with a moving object and a shutter speed of ¹/₆₀ second is used, the object will remain sharp but the background will be blurred. This technique is called panning.

● LEFT By contrast, a shutter speed of ¹/₂₅₀ second was used to photograph this bird in flight, and it has 'frozen' virtually all movement.

Most cameras today have built-in exposure metering systems. These should enable the photographer to get the correct exposure every time. However, in many situations the metering system is led astray by the general level of light, so that the subject of the photograph is over- or underexposed. This is because many systems take an average reading of the illumination over the whole frame. If you are photographing a person against a white wall, or if there is a lot of sky in the frame, these big light areas will have the greatest influence on the meter. Unless you compensate for this the person will come out underexposed, in extreme cases reduced to a silhouette. Conversely, if you place a person against a dark background the metering system will read mainly for this area, and if you do not make an adjustment the person will come out overexposed.

THE AUTOMATIC EXPOSURE LOCK

This problem can be resolved by using the camera's automatic exposure lock. This sets itself when the shutter release is lightly pressed. It holds the current exposure setting until the release is pressed to fire the shutter, or until the button is released altogether. So you can go up close to your subject, take an accurate reading from their flesh tones, hold down the shutter release and go back to your chosen viewpoint for the

● ABOVE Bracketing exposures lets you make slight variations in exposure that may make all the difference to the final picture. In this case the difference was ⅓ of a stop between each one. Here, TOP, the meter gave a reading that has slightly underexposed the girl, making her eyes look heavy and dark.

With the aperture increased slightly, MIDDLE, the skin tones are more natural and the shadowiness of the eyes has been eliminated.

A further increase in the exposure has made the facial features begin to burn out. So the picture on the BOTTOM would be chosen for the final print.

composition. If you want to take several shots you will have to follow the same procedure for each one.

SPOT METERING

If your camera has a variable metering system, you can use spot metering in such cases. This restricts the meter to measuring the light falling on a small spot in the centre of the viewfinder.

USING A HAND-HELD METER

There are two main ways of taking a reading with a hand-held meter:
● For a reflected light reading, point the meter at the subject and take a reading of the light reflected from it.
● For an incident light reading, place a small white disc, or invercone, over the meter cell. Some meters have a white blind which can be slid over the cell. Hold the meter against the subject and point it back towards the camera. This gives a more accurate reading of the light falling on the subject.

BRACKETING

Another way of getting the correct exposure is to bracket. For example, imagine that the metering system is giving a reading of ¹⁄₁₂₅ at f8. If you take one shot at this setting, one slightly over it and one slightly under, when the film is processed you can judge which exposure has worked best and make a print from that negative.

● ABOVE The camera meter took an average reading. As there was so much sky, which even on a dull day is bright in comparison to other areas of the picture, the girl has come out underexposed. ABOVE RIGHT Going in close and using the camera's exposure lock has given a truer reading of the flesh tones and a far more flattering exposure.

● RIGHT Spot metering has given an accurate exposure of the girl. If your camera does not have this feature you will have to use the exposure lock or a hand-held meter.

GENERAL COMPOSITION

Cameras are becoming increasingly sophisticated with their built-in exposure metering systems, and it would seem to follow that the photographer has more time to concentrate on areas such as composition. However, this is often not the case. Unwanted intrusions confuse and distract the eye; backgrounds that are irrelevant or dominating overpower the foreground, and foregrounds that should lead the eye into the picture either occupy too great an area or appear merely because of incorrect framing. All these faults can be corrected with very little effort and only minimal preparation.

● ABOVE Even when a photographic opportunity occurs by chance, it pays to take time to consider the general composition. Here the chess board fills the centre of the foreground and the two subjects are positioned on either side, creating a perfect balance. The scene captures a particular image of society, especially with the inclusion of the third man in the background; although not deliberately arranged, the three people and the juxtaposed chess board have become key elements in the final photograph.

● ABOVE This very simple shot has all the ingredients of a good composition. The foreground is uncluttered, and the pathway leads from the foreground directly to the centre of interest, the house. The house is set against a backdrop of small hills, which do not overpower the house but provide a contrast and add interest by breaking up the uniform stretch of blue sky.

● ABOVE This nutseller is the centre of interest and as such occupies the middle position in the shot. Do not be afraid of placing the subject in a prominent position within the frame of the picture. Here the subject sits ' among a display of his wares; this helps draw the eye towards him yet also around him as more and more items become apparent. Always retain an even balance between the subject and his surroundings.

● RIGHT The arch in the foreground provides a natural frame for this scene in a church in Moscow. This arch is complemented by a series of other arches that can be seen in the background as the eye travels from one to the other in a smooth sequence. There are no unsightly intrusions in either the foreground or background. This is a strong composition which may well have been weaker if taken from a different viewpoint.

THREE KEY AREAS TO BE CONSIDERED IN COMPOSITION:

1 The centre of interest – having decided what the central subject of the photograph is to be, ascertain where the photograph is to be shot from to achieve the most effective background.

2 Possible distractions or intrusions – examine carefully the subject, background and foreground to ensure the picture will not be spoilt by an unwanted object. It is only too easy to mar a beautiful building with a traffic sign in the foreground, or to produce a portrait of some friends complete with a telegraph pole emerging from the top of one of their heads. Usually an intruding object can be removed from the composition simply by moving slightly to one side. It is worth waiting for any moving vehicles to pass by.

3 Enhancing the foreground – it is important to decide if there is anything that might add to the foreground without detracting from or obscuring the centre of interest.

USING FOREGROUND

Foregrounds can play an important part in the general composition of photographs. A point of interest in the foreground close to the camera can be used either as a framing device or as a tool to lead the eye into the picture. This type of added interest can make all the difference between the exciting and the mediocre.

USING FOREGROUND AS A DISGUISE

Foregrounds can also be used to hide untidy objects or unwanted intrusions in the middle or background of the picture. However, it is important to make sure that the foreground does not dominate the picture as then it will detract from the main subject of the photograph, becoming as much of an intrusion as the detail it is attempting to disguise.

OBJECTS IN THE FOREGROUND

Although objects in the foreground of a picture can add interest, it is all too easy to let them appear with monotonous regularity. This is a danger with a series of pictures taken from similar viewpoints, yet can be easily avoided with a little thought. Take time to evaluate what is in front of the camera; use all the components to their best advantage in the final shot.

When objects are included in the foreground care must be taken with the exposure. Check to see if the objects are in shadow compared to the central portion of the shot and background as this may produce an ugly dark shape with no detail visible. If the shadow is unavoidable try correcting it using a reflector or fill-in flash.

Also check to see if the camera needs to be higher than the object in the foreground. If not, make sure the object is not filling too much of the frame.

● LEFT This picture of a formal garden has been enhanced by the use of the foliage of the outer trees as a framing device. The gates at the bottom of the frame complete the foreground interest. The result gives the impression of peering into a 'secret' garden. If the camera had been positioned further forward and the foreground lost, the picture would have looked entirely different.

USE OF PERSPECTIVE TO CREATE FOREGROUND INTEREST

Additional foreground interest can be created by the use of perspective, for example the furrows in a ploughed field stretching out into the distance. In this case, a low viewpoint might be best. When taking a landscape shot the sky can often be a dominating factor so that the landscape scene itself is overpowered. If this happens, perhaps the addition of a tree with overhanging branches within the shot could frame the top of the picture and diminish the impact of the sky.

● ABOVE Not all historical buildings are always at their best – as here in Reims, France, where the cathedral was covered in scaffolding. Added to this the early-morning sun rose behind the cathedral and since there was no time to wait for the sun's position to alter a viewpoint was found some distance from the front of the building. A telephoto lens, 200 mm, was used and by having as a framing device the trees in the foreground the untidy scaffolding was concealed and the direct sunlight was blocked.

● ABOVE Foreground objects do not always need to be placed dead centre. Here the boat is in the bottom right-hand corner of the frame and creates an added degree of foreground interest. The colour of the boat complements the colour of the lush green grass without providing too harsh a contrast. If a picture of this sort is to be part of a series, try to vary the position of the object in the foreground so that it does not become a dull motif, detracting from the shots themselves.

● ABOVE The strong lines of the strata shoot out from the foreground and pierce the sea, leading the eye straight into the picture and creating a powerful composition. If the photograph had been taken from a position at the end of the rocks, the foreground would have been merely a dull stretch of sea with no added interest.

USING BACKGROUND

The background of a picture can enhance the overall composition of an image in ways similar to the effects of the foreground. As a general rule, backgrounds should not dominate the photograph, obscuring the main subject. This jars the eye and gives an overall impression of a cluttered photograph. Similarly, a flat, dull background can influence the whole picture so that all interest is lost. A telephoto lens can produce a compressed image, bringing the background forward and reducing the depth between the middle- and foreground.

The weather can create dramatic effects; if dark clouds are hanging in the sky watch out for isolated bursts of sunlight which can spotlight areas of the foreground, underexposing and making the dark areas even darker.

When taking a shot of an apparently tranquil landscape, check to see if there are any roads or tracks running through. If there are, wait until traffic has dispersed as an unsightly track can ruin an otherwise beautiful scene.

● ABOVE LEFT The cows form an almost monochromatic background to this picture. The track that comes down to the gate balances the picture and enhances the general composition, yet nothing detracts from the young girl. Her bright raincoat and hat are set off by the black and white cows, and the juxtaposition of her diminutive size alongside the cows adds a subtle touch of humour to the shot.

● ABOVE RIGHT The ever-burning flame of this oil refinery on the banks of the Mississippi at New Orleans relieves an otherwise dull background. It also provides a powerful contrast with the more traditional technology of the old paddle steamer in the foreground. It always pays to be alert to pictures where the back- and foregrounds provide not only a visual contrast but can also make a wider abstract statement in visual terms.

● RIGHT This picture was taken using only the available light coming in through a small window and with an exposure of ⅛ second, bracing the camera against the bar. It is a clear example of how the background can provide information about the subject while at the same time adding extra interest and detail.

● LEFT This salmon fisherman is holding a putcher, a funnel-shaped basket used to catch salmon as they swim out to sea. The stakes stretching out behind echo the mood of the putcher, and convey a greater sense of the man and his work.

KEY POINTS TO NOTE ABOUT BACKGROUNDS:

1 Is the background overpowering? Will it overshadow the subject of the picture? On the other hand, does it have enough interest to prevent it from being dull?

2 Does the background behind a human subject represent anything about the person's work or environment?

3 Are the background colours harmonious or unusual in some way? A telephoto lens can push the background out of focus, throwing up some interesting shapes and muted colours.

4 Does the sky appear in the background? If there are any clouds, try to retain their clarity and detail, perhaps by using a graduated neutral density filter or polarizing filter, or a yellow filter with black and white film.

CHOOSING A VIEWPOINT

There are many situations when taking a photograph where a simple alteration of viewpoint can make all the difference. Viewpoint can be defined as the position from which a photograph is taken, and takes into account the background and foreground, and any interesting angles that will lead the eye naturally towards the emphasis of the image. By using different viewpoints the photographer can dramatically alter the impact of a picture.

Often people will say to a professional photographer something along the lines of, 'But you've got all the equipment!' In fact, all that it takes to achieve a better view is a little thought of where one should stand and how the foreground can be utilized to the greatest effect. On many occasions it may be possible to utilize detail in the foreground by either tilting the camera downward or by moving slightly to one side. These small shifts of position or angle, that may seem insignificant at the time, can produce the difference between the dramatic and the dull.

● BELOW The choice of lens is important for the composition of a picture.

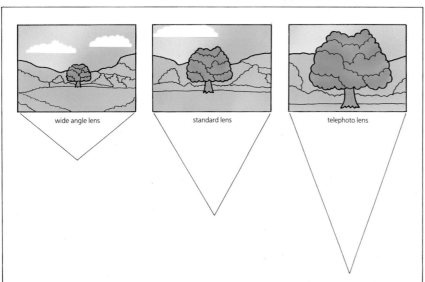

wide angle lens   standard lens   telephoto lens

● ABOVE AND INSET Viewed individually there may seem little to choose between these two pictures of Brooklyn Bridge. The shots were taken within 46 m (150 ft) of one another and within a short space of time. The upper picture was taken from further away than the lower one; much of its impact is lost by the inclusion of too much sky at the top of the frame, and the cloud is an added distraction.

The lower picture was taken from much nearer to the bridge using a slightly lower viewpoint. This means that the verticals have converged to a greater degree than they would have done had the shot been taken from a higher position, and the tension cables fill the frame, fanning out in all directions to draw the eye into the shot. The cloud has been cropped out which extends the symmetry of the shot; with fewer distractions the graphic qualities of the composition are enhanced.

EASY ESTIMATING

To help judge your choice of viewpoint, simply form a rectangle between the thumbs and forefingers of both hands, and look through to judge your chosen image.

To tighten the 'frame', slide the right hand closer to the left, keeping the rectangle steady. In order to create a 'zoom' effect, extend your arms so that the background is removed and the

subject of the picture appears larger in relation to the rectangle.

● ABOVE Standing close to one element of a photograph can add extra emphasis. The viewpoint for this picture was created by standing close to the canyon wall that appears on the left. The dramatic sweep of the wall and its horizontal strata lead the eye straight into the picture. If taken from a different position or angle the effect would have been weaker.

● RIGHT By tilting the camera downward the lilies on the water are brought into the picture. This provides extra interest in the foreground without detracting from the mountains and sky beyond. If the camera had been horizontal or tilted upward slightly, without including the lilies, the result would have been a rather dull stretch of water and reflected cloud in the foreground.

Daylight colour film, as its name suggests, is for use with daylight-lit subjects or with electronic flash. If daylight film is used indoors where the main source of illumination is provided by domestic light bulbs, the resulting pictures will have a predominantly orange cast to them. This is because what is known as the 'colour temperature' of the light source would be at variance with the colour balance of the film.

COLOUR TEMPERATURE

Colour temperature is usually measured in values of kelvin. To achieve the correct balance when using daylight film in artificial light of 3200 kelvin requires the use of an 80A filter. This is a blue-coloured filter which corrects the orange cast that is otherwise created. However, the blue-coloured filter is quite a dense filter and will cut down the amount of light passing through the lens onto the film; to compensate for this, 64 ISO film must be rated at 16 ISO. Care must be taken when adjusting for these factors as a long exposure is needed – yet most daylight-balanced colour film suffers from reciprocity failure at exposures of 1 second or longer.

When you expose daylight-balanced colour film for exposures of longer than approximately 1 second, the film will suffer from reciprocity failure i.e. where the stated ISO rating no longer applies. An example of this is where a 100 ISO film may only be 25 ISO at an exposure of 10 seconds. Owing to the unpredictable nature of the film in these circumstances, the only sure way of getting the right exposure is to test the film in the prevailing light conditions to see what ISO it should be rated at.

When using tungsten-balanced colour reversal films and the few tungsten-balanced colour negative films available these problems are solved. There is no need to add a filter to the camera when shooting in situations where the colour temperature is 3200 kelvin, and tungsten-balanced film can be used at far longer exposures than daylight film without suffering from reciprocity failure.

If daylight-balanced colour negative film is used in tungsten light it can always be corrected at printing stage. If daylight-balanced colour reversal film is used in tungsten light without an 80A filter the resulting transparencies would have to be duplicated and corrected at the printing stage. This is expensive, and, however good the duplicates are, some of the quality will inevitably be lost.

● TOP LEFT If daylight-balanced colour film is used in artificial light the results will have an orange cast. To correct this imbalance an 80A filter needs to be used, TOP RIGHT. Alternatively, tungsten-balanced film used in artificial light does not require a colour-balanced filter.

● BOTTOM LEFT Using tungsten film in daylight or with electronic flash will result in pictures with a blue cast. To correct this, use an 85B filter, BOTTOM RIGHT. As an alternative, use daylight-balanced film in daylight or with electronic flash as this does not need a colour-balanced filter.

● ABOVE When shooting in artificial light it is often necessary to use long exposures. This picture required the shutter to be open for 30 seconds. Since the lighting was tungsten, tungsten-balanced colour film was used. Apart from the fact that it rendered the colour correctly, tungsten film suffers far less from reciprocity failure than daylight-balanced film.

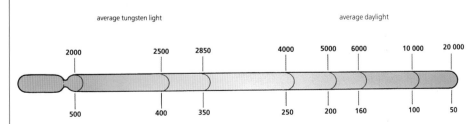

average tungsten light   average daylight

| 2000 | | 2500 | 2850 | | 4000 | 5000 | 6000 | 10 000 | 20 000 |
| 500 | | 400 | 350 | | 250 | 200 | 160 | 100 | 50 |

● LEFT Light is measured in values of kelvin. The measurements change according to the type of light, from warm to cool.

SHOOTING IN MIXED LIGHT

Occasionally there are situations, especially indoors, when the light comes from many different light sources. These light sources may all have different colour temperatures, so using just tungsten-balanced film or filtering daylight-balanced film to 3200 kelvin may not be adequate.

FLUORESCENT LIGHT

One of the most difficult lights to balance is fluorescent light. This is because there are many different types of fluorescent light tubes ranging from cool to warm white. When a tube wears out it might be replaced with a tube of a different colour temperature. To the naked eye, all the tubes may look the same yet they are in fact giving off different temperatures of colour which makes choosing the correct filter very difficult.

DAYLIGHT MIXED WITH ARTIFICIAL LIGHT

Sometimes with two different light sources, such as tungsten light and daylight or fluorescent light and daylight, the only practical solution may be to expose for the greater light source. A more elaborate method – when shooting in a room lit by tungsten light with windows that let in daylight – is to place light-balancing material over the windows to convert the daylight to the same balance as the tungsten light.

In mixed light situations that combine daylight with tungsten, the warmth of the tungsten light can add a mellow tone. If the situation is one which combines daylight, tungsten and flash, the trick is to make all of these elements balance. The best method to achieve this is to work out the exposure for the daylight coming in through the windows. For example, it may be 1 second at f16. If so, adjust the power of the flash to give an exposure of f16. (Shooting at speeds slower than the flash setting on the camera will not alter the flash exposure; this will only happen if a faster speed is used than is recommended for the camera.) Set the shutter speed to 1 second and take the shot. At this exposure tungsten light (coming, for example, from a table lamp) will be recorded without causing an unnatural colour cast.

● ABOVE In the TOP shot daylight predominates and the picture comes out well on the daylight film in the camera. BOTTOM, using the same film and pointing the camera down to a small area of the building lit by tungsten light without the use of an 80A filter has created a definite orange cast.

● LEFT This picture, taken outdoors at dusk, shows several different light sources but because of the expanse of the picture and its varied elements it appears correctly exposed even though the lights have differing colour balances.

● ABOVE This picture of the famous food halls of Harrods in London is a good example of a mixed light situation: the ceramic well set into the ceiling is lit by fluorescent lighting yet the rest of the store is lit by tungsten. In the time available it was impossible to put colour correction gels over all the fluorescent tubes so a compromise had to be reached. Since the fluorescent light was illuminating an isolated area, the whole shot was exposed for tungsten.

● FAR LEFT This museum room has fluorescent light as the dominant source which has given the shot a green cast. LEFT An FLD (fluorescent daylight) filter removes this and adds a natural tone.

USING FLASH

Flash has become as commonplace as the cameras that use it. It provides a convenient, renewable, instant and often adjustable extra light source. Some cameras have built-in flash while other models take flash unit attachments. Professional photographers use large free-standing flash units for studio work yet excellent results can be obtained with less expensive equipment.

BUILT-IN FLASH

Built-in flash is very convenient, yet like any piece of equipment it has its drawbacks. The flash tends to be rather weak and any subject beyond approximately 10 ft (3 m) will be underexposed. The output of the flash may be constant and no adjustment available; the disadvantage of this is that anything very close to the flash will be burnt out. The most common problem is that of 'red eye'. 'Red eye' occurs when the flash is fired near the axis of the lens. If a shot is taken of a person looking at the camera, the flash will bounce off the retina of the eye and produce a red spot in the final picture. The remedy is to move the flash away from the axis of the lens. This cannot be done with built-in flash. If the flash is of the type that flashes several times in quick succession when the shutter release button is depressed, finally firing at full strength, the pupil of the eye contracts so that there is less of the retina from which the flash can be reflected and it does not appear red.

SEPARATE FLASH UNITS

Separate flash units may be more powerful than built-in flash. They are attached to the camera hot shoe or to a special bracket and sync lead. Many units have heads that can be angled upwards to varying degrees so that the light can be bounced off a ceiling or

● TOP LEFT Using a flash gun attached to the side of the camera creates a harsh light with a shadow to one side.

● BOTTOM LEFT Placing a diffuser over the flash softens the shadow but it is still quite obvious.

● TOP RIGHT By moving the flash even further to one side the shadow is accentuated.

● BOTTOM RIGHT By bouncing the light off the ceiling the shadow on the wall has been eliminated, but at the expense of a shadow under the chin.

other pale material. If this type of angled flash is used for a portrait the light will be softer but might result in dark shadows under the eyes, nose and chin. These can be avoided by using fill-in flash.

FILL-IN FLASH

A built-in fill-in flash unit is positioned under the main flash attachment. When the flash is fired on 'bounce mode' with the fill-in flash, 80 per cent of the power passes through the main flash while the remaining 20 per cent goes through the fill-in unit. This removes most of the shadows from under the eyes, nose and chin. Another method of softening flash light is to diffuse it. This can be done very simply by placing a small cloth such as a handkerchief over the flash, or even by holding a piece of tracing paper just in front of the flash itself.

● TOP LEFT Sometimes daylight is not enough even though a built-in meter may advise you to the contrary.

● BOTTOM LEFT Fill-in balanced flash helps eliminate the problem by bringing the exposure required for the person to the same level as that required for the background.

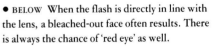
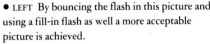

● BELOW When the flash is directly in line with the lens, a bleached-out face often results. There is always the chance of 'red eye' as well.

● LEFT By bouncing the flash in this picture and using a fill-in flash as well a more acceptable picture is achieved.

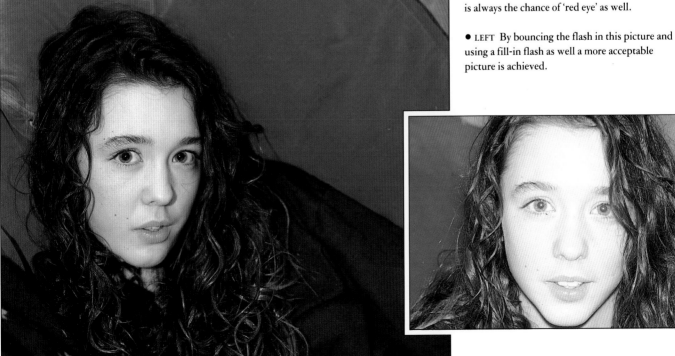

USING WIDE ANGLE LENSES

Additional lenses are the accessories that will probably do the most to improve your photography. A wide angle lens offers you a completely different perspective on a traditional view. Not only will its wider angle of view get more into the picture, but it also has a greater depth of field than a normal or telephoto lens, so that more of the shot will be sharp.

You can have an object relatively close to the lens and still keep the background in focus. If the object is close enough it will look much larger in proportion to the rest of the picture than it really is. With extreme wide angle lenses, distortion can be a problem and you should not photograph people from too close in, to avoid unflattering results. For instance, a 21 mm lens pointed directly at someone's face will make the nose look enormous, the cheeks puffed out, and the ears as if they have moved round towards the back of their head. This might be fun at first, but the novelty will soon wear off and it will be time to turn to more serious applications.

● ABOVE The impact of this shot relies on the feeling of the 'big' landscape. The wide field of view gives a feeling of overwhelming space and loneliness. The lines marked on the road exaggerate the already strong perspective and give the impression that the road goes on endlessly.

● RIGHT Using a low viewpoint with a wide angle lens makes it look as if the windmill sails are soaring into the sky. The great depth of field offered by the lens makes the whole picture sharp even though the bottom of the sail is quite close to the lens. It is very important to choose the correct viewpoint when using a lens of this kind.

● **LEFT** A drought has dried up this lake, exposing an old tree stump. Again, the wide angle lens keeps the whole picture sharp. Placing the stump at one side of the frame gives it an almost living quality, as if it is walking towards what remains of the lake.

● **RIGHT** When photographing people, take great care to avoid unflattering distortion. In this picture, although the hands and arms are distorted this is within tolerable limits and does not unbalance the composition as the viewpoint and angle of the shot have been carefully chosen. Although the arms look long and the hands, which are closest to the lens, enormous, the imbalance is acceptable because the strong hands represent the nature of the fisherman's work. His arms lead the eye straight to his face, which is framed in turn by a backdrop of his working environment. The busy background keeps the eye from dwelling too long on his hands so that, large as they are, they simply appear to be part of the composition.

USING TELEPHOTO LENSES

Telephoto lenses do much more than just bring distant objects closer. They can greatly enhance general composition. Their shallow depth of field can blur the background in a portrait to isolate and emphasize the subject. In contrast to wide angle lenses, going in close to people has a positively flattering effect. This is because a telephoto lens slightly compresses the picture so that prominent features such as the nose and ears stay in proportion. Careful use of a telephoto lens can also help to cut out unwanted foreground clutter, allowing you to get to the heart of the picture.

EXPOSURE AND APERTURE SETTINGS

Some compensation has to be made in settings when using a telephoto lens, especially a long one. This is because the magnifying effect of the lens spreads the available light out more thinly, and the longer the lens the greater the effect. With cameras that have TTL metering this is no problem, but a manual camera will have to be adjusted.

Telephoto lenses also tend to have smaller apertures than normal or wide angle lenses, so that exposure must be longer. There are exceptions: some of the latest telephoto lenses have apertures as big as f2.8, but these lenses are very expensive, and few amateur photographers will consider that their usefulness justifies the price. If you need a fast long lens for a particular shot it would be more sensible to hire one.

USING A TRIPOD

The image made by a telephoto lens shifts very rapidly when the camera is moved. This fact together with the long exposure time may call for the use of a tripod or monopod. With a lens over 300 mm this will be essential: it is almost impossible to hold the camera still enough to avoid shake and a blurred image.

CONVERTERS

You would need to use a very long lens such as a 500 mm very often to justify its high price. If not, you might consider using a converter. This fits between the camera body and an existing lens. A 2 x converter will increase the focal length of a 250 mm lens to 500 mm. The price is reasonable and the image almost as sharp as that of a long lens. Most camera manufacturers make converters.

● This was shot with a 28 mm wide angle lens. It has stretched the telephone boxes apart and given a very elongated effect.

● Here a 135 mm telephoto lens has been used. It has compressed the boxes so that they look closer together. The composition is far tighter and cuts out much unwanted detail from the frame.

● RIGHT The use of a 200 mm telephoto lens has cropped a lot of clutter out of the picture. The lens has compressed the picture, reducing the apparent space between buildings. Such a composition emphasizes the contrasts between the various architectural styles, from the Victorian classical façade to the modern skyscrapers in the background.

● BELOW A 100 mm telephoto lens is ideal for portraiture. Its short depth of field, especially at wide apertures, can put the background out of focus and thus allow the viewer to concentrate on the main subject. In such shots it is best to focus on the eyes and expose for the skin tones.

INSTANT OR POLAROID CAMERAS

Polaroid cameras are unique among cameras as they provide an instant print within a few minutes. The prints can be either colour or black and white and begin to develop as soon as the film sheet appears from the camera; the sheets are impregnated with developing chemicals activated by pressure. Reprints can be made from the originals if they are sent away and copied. These, like the film itself, can be expensive.

The variety of Polaroids available range from the inexpensive 'point-and-shoot' models to those that have interchangeable lenses, built-in metering and flash. In the mid-price range is the image system; this has autoexposure, autofocusing and built-in flash, together with a range of accessories including a close-up lens. The film used in the image system model is supplied with a built-in battery that powers the camera: every time the film is replaced the battery is also renewed.

POLAROID BACKS

As well as the conventional camera unit, Polaroid backs which fit onto a range of more traditional cameras from 35 mm SLRs to large format 5 × 4s are also available. These backs allow the photographer to view the composition and make adjustments before taking the final shot on conventional film. The lighting can be checked and corrected if necessary and the exposure assessed. Prints can be collected and displayed in an album as a visual and technical record of how a shot was taken; this is especially useful as a reference when a similar composition is needed again.

Some of the film used in Polaroid backs produces a negative as well as a print. This means that it is not necessary to obtain copies from prints, where quality may be lost.

October - Lucy's birthday party

The Gang

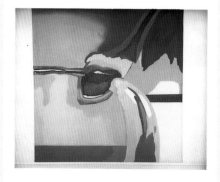

The prizewinning entry!

The leaves beginning to turn

Signor Serafino at the restaurant

Surprise, Surprise!

Almost perfect symmetry!

Mr Jackson and chemistry class

Tiger looking fierce

Tom and Jim in the park

Waiting for the furniture to arrive

A balcony shot of Sarah's party

Dinah posing for her portrait

The happy couple

A lucky snap - the portico background matches the sky

UNDERSTANDING AUTOFOCUS

Many compact cameras now have an autofocus facility built in; this allows for even more spontaneity in instant shots. The autofocus camera emits an invisible infrared beam which bounces back off the subject to the camera in much the same way that radar works. The camera analyses this information and sets the focus to the correct distance by means of a small electric motor.

It sounds simple and it is, but there are a few points to remember before shooting the picture. On the most simple autofocus cameras the area analysed by the autofocus mechanism will be in the centre of the frame; it will be this part that the camera focuses on even if the main subject is to one side and therefore out of the autofocus range. It is very simple to learn how to alter the focus by manually overriding this mechanism.

Some of the more sophisticated cameras have a larger area of focus than that of the central spot found in the more simple models. These more sophisticated cameras send out three separate beams and make a 'judgement', either from one of these or from a combination. Many of the single lens reflex cameras that take interchangeable lenses are now of the autofocusing type. Most of these have a manual override for focusing but when in the autofocus mode the same alterations may be required.

1 Shutter release button
– this may also include a pre-set focus control to allow overriding of the autofocus mechanism

4 Autofocus windows
– these send out an infrared beam to judge the focusing requirements of a picture

6 Self-timer indicator lamp
– a blinking light that speeds up as the shutter is about to be released

2 Multifunction LCD and mode controls
– a display panel and controls to measure and adjust additional flash requirements and the self-timer

3 Flash
– this charges up almost instantly and may include a blinking anti-red-eye device

5 Auto exposure metering window
– a light measuring device which judges the amount of light and any flash requirements; some models have a 'spot' reading mechanism

7 Viewfinder
– this gives an accurate visual image of the photograph about to be taken

8 Lens
– this can contain both an autofocus and a zoom facility, allowing for variety in depth of the image

• In this shot the person is in the centre of the frame and is perfectly sharp. The background is out of focus as the automatic focusing mechanism has 'fixed' onto the subject in the foreground. Perhaps the subject needs to be moved to one side in order to reveal or conceal part of the background.

• By repositioning the camera so that the person is at one side of the picture the background comes into sharp focus but the girl is now blurred.

• To eliminate the problem is quite simple. First point the camera at the person and gently depress the shutter release button to a half-way position. This will fix the autofocus mechanism on the subject in the foreground. Keeping the shutter release button depressed, move the camera to the desired position so that the picture is composed satisfactorily. Now depress the shutter release button fully. The picture has now been taken and the person is in focus.

• BELOW Autofocus is excellent for capturing instant and spontaneous shots that retain the essence of a particular moment.

ADVANTAGES OF AUTOMATIC CAMERAS

• Automatic focusing allows spontaneous pictures to be captured instantly without time-consuming dial adjustments.

• The built-in flash provides quick, on-the-spot lighting for every occasion.

• Light exposure is metered automatically, saving on adjustment and measuring time.

• 'Hands-free' pictures can be taken using the self-timer; even the photographer can appear in the shot.

• The small, compact shape makes the camera easily portable in all situations.

WHEN THINGS GO WRONG

Even when you think you have taken every possible care with your photography, things can still go disappointingly wrong. Often these errors are caused by a momentary lapse of concentration, but in extreme cases the fault can be traced to a malfunction in the camera or other equipment.

Do not be discouraged by faults in your photography; problems are nearly always easy to rectify. Look at the examples shown here and compare your own pictures to diagnose and correct the fault.

Probably the most common fault is fogging of the film. This occurs when the camera back is opened before the film has been fully rewound into the cassette, or because light is leaking into the camera. If light is leaking in, take the camera to a reputable repairer.

If the film is blank when it comes back from the processors, the most likely fault is that the film has not been advancing. When you load the camera, always check to make sure the rewind crank turns when you advance the film; if it does not turn, the film will stay in the cassette.

Consistent overexposure of film may be caused by a defective meter. However, it may also occur if the wrong speed is set or the metering system is set to the wrong ISO speed. Alternatively, this may take place if the aperture on the lens is not stopping down when the shot is taken; this means that the lens needs repairing.

Blurred shots are usually caused by camera shake. This will occur if you are using a slow shutter speed without securing the camera to a tripod. If the camera has aperture priority mode and you are shooting in dull light, the camera will select a slow shutter speed if you choose a small aperture.

● Flash overexposure. Cause: the sensor that determines the power of the flash was covered by part of a hand. To correct: always leave the sensor clear.

● Flare and marks on the film. Cause: after loading, the film has not been wound on two or three frames before shooting begins. The laboratory's processing marks and number are visible over the image. To correct: always be sure to wind on the film for at least a couple of frames before beginning photography.

● Incorrect framing. Cause: parallax error. When shooting with a compact camera the viewfinder does not see exactly what the lens sees. To correct: refer to the manufacturer's parallax adjustment guide.

● Out of focus. Cause: going too close or incorrect use of an autofocus mechanism so that the middle distance is measured, in this case the plants behind the subject. To correct: semi-depress the shutter on the main foreground subject before framing the shot.

● ABOVE Under-exposure. Cause: the auto-exposure meter has read the reading from the sky rather than from the person. To correct: be sure to take a reading from the main subject.

● ABOVE Marks on prints. Cause: the camera back was opened before the film was wound back into the cassette. To correct: ensure the cassette is fully rewound before opening the camera back.

● ABOVE 'Red eye'. Cause: the flash is too close to the lens. To correct: move the flash to one side if possible, or activate the anti-red-eye flash mechanism if one is fitted.

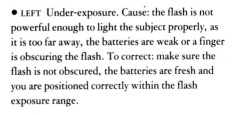

● ABOVE Over-exposed background. Cause: the auto-exposure meter in the camera has taken a reading for the trees in the foreground and over-exposed for the background. To correct: ensure the readings are taken from the main area of interest.

● ABOVE Murky print. Cause: the camera case or a hand is obscuring part of the lens. To correct: ensure the lens is never obstructed.

● LEFT Under-exposure. Cause: the flash is not powerful enough to light the subject properly, as it is too far away, the batteries are weak or a finger is obscuring the flash. To correct: make sure the flash is not obscured, the batteries are fresh and you are positioned correctly within the flash exposure range.

Travel Photography

INTRODUCTION

Going on holiday, especially abroad, provides the photographer with many different sights and renewed creative energy. Not only are there new geographical vistas to be shot but also local people and colourful environments. Unusual architecture and local or national parades and carnivals also provide a wealth of possibilities. Although it is true that travel to foreign and faraway places can prove to be inspirational there are many exciting photographic opportunities nearer to home as well. A few simple basics and a good eye are all that is needed to get the best out of photography — whether it is around the corner or half-way around the world.

TRAVEL PREPARED

Before travelling away from home, especially for a holiday, collect together all the photographic equipment needed to record the journey. Do not try to take every piece of equipment and all additional lenses, lighting and accessories: just take enough to cover most situations.

HOLIDAY CHECKLIST

● How long have the batteries been in the camera? Do they need replacing? Make sure spares are packed; it is still difficult to find certain types of battery in some countries. If the camera uses rechargeable batteries, be sure to pack the charger, together with an international plug converter.

● Take one or two zoom lenses; these will cover most of the focal lengths required and will save on the weight and space that a number of prime lenses would take up.

● Two camera bodies will mean faster work as the time taken to change lenses will be reduced; one camera could be fitted with a 28–80 mm lens and the other with a 100–300 mm lens.

● Consider having black and white film in one camera and colour in the other; alternatively try loading one body with fast film and the other with slow.

● Try to purchase all film likely to be needed from a reputable supplier before leaving. The film will be fresh and probably cheaper. In some countries it is difficult to obtain very fresh film, and in hot climates it may have been on a shelf in bright sunshine. If you are concerned about it passing through the X-ray security machine at an airport there are protective bags available from specialist shops.

● Think about taking one or two filters; an 81A will help add a little warmth to the pictures, while a

polarizing filter will enhance the quality of the sky and sea while also cutting down on or eliminating unwanted reflections. A graduated neutral density filter will help balance the areas of the picture that require different exposures, for instance a bright sky above a dark landscape. A yellow filter when used with black and white film will help retain the clarity of clouds.

● A flash gun is useful in cases where the light is low as well as in bright sun

as a fill-in light. As with the camera, make sure the batteries are fresh and that a spare supply is packed.

● A small portable reflector is an asset, especially for portraits.

● It is worth taking a tripod, together with a cable release. If the tripod is too

● Take everything you are likely to need for a trip. This camera case contains the essential items for travel photography: a compact but sturdy tripod, a variety of film for colour as well as black and white shots, a camera body and lenses, and filters and flash equipment. Always check everything thoroughly before setting off on your travels, and remember to pack spare batteries!

bulky, consider a monopod instead.
● Lens cleaning tissue and a blower brush are essential, especially in sandy or dusty locations. Wrap the camera in a plastic bag to protect it from dust or sand particles, and as a general measure against the effects of the environment and extreme weather conditions.
● A camera case to hold all this equipment is extremely useful; when travelling by air and not keeping the case as hand luggage, it is best to have a hard aluminium case for maximum protection.

WHEN THE LIGHT IS LOW

Low light, whether due to the time of day or prevailing weather conditions, does not mean that good photographs cannot be taken. It is sometimes even possible to obtain more dramatic shots in low light than in brilliant sunshine. If the weather is misty or foggy, moody pictures can be taken. If the sun is low, at the beginning or end of the day, for instance, the colour of the light will be much warmer, and can be used to dramatic advantage, emphasizing the sky and clouds. Even indoors, light filtering through a window is often perfectly adequate to light a subject without using flash.

A tripod is an asset in many low light conditions where slow shutter speeds are necessary. An alternative is to use a fast film, although the results will be grainier. Graininess can be used to creative effect but often it will detract from the final image if not used carefully. Instead of using fast film, ordinary film can be uprated. If the film in the camera is 100 ISO, for instance, the speed dial on the camera can be altered to 200 or 400 ISO. Remember, though, to tell the laboratory this when the film is sent in for processing so that it can be developed accordingly. The disadvantage of this method is that the whole film has to be rated at the same ISO and any increase in development will result in loss of shadow detail, increase in contrast and a grainier texture.

● BELOW The late evening light bathes this building in a wonderful reddish glow. The anonymous figure at the window lends an air of mystery to the overall composition. Always be on the look-out for the unexpected, especially when the light is low and hopes of a good shot are fading.

● ABOVE This shot was taken using only available light coming in from a window. The shutter speed required was $1/15$ second; this was too slow to allow the camera to be held by hand so a column in the restaurant was used as a support. It is virtually impossible to hold a camera steady at $1/30$ second or less without suffering camera shake; with a little ingenuity it is usually possible to find something to support the camera.

● RIGHT Here the setting sun has painted the sky completely red and the clouds lend it extra depth. No tripod was available here so the camera was braced on the defensive wall of the river.

● LEFT Even adverse weather conditions can be used to the photographer's advantage. This picture of Bodiam Castle in Great Britain was taken early on a misty morning. The mist rose and fell, sometimes completely obscuring the castle. By waiting for the right moment it was possible to take a shot in which the light had an ethereal quality. The mirror image reflected in the still waters of the moat adds to the general composition.

Any accessory used while taking a photograph can enhance the final image; however, care must always be taken to ensure the images produced are effective. One of the least expensive and yet most important of accessories is a filter. Certain filters improve the colour saturation of the film or enhance the sky or quality of water. Before deciding on any filter, indeed any accessory, test it in similar situations before using it for a specific shot.

COLOUR CORRECTION FILTERS

Some manufacturers' film may have a natural bias towards results that are too blue or green, giving an unwanted coldness to the photographs. On the other hand, the film may be too warm and the results will then tend towards red or yellow. To correct these tendencies there is a huge range of CC (colour correction) filters; for most photographers one or two colour balancing filters will prove more than adequate.

POLARIZING FILTERS

A polarizing filter is a useful accessory; not only will it enhance the quality of the blueness of a sky, making any clouds stand out with greater clarity, it can also be used to cut out unwanted reflections, such as those in shop windows or on shiny tabletops.

EXPOSURE COMPENSATION

Since many filters cut down the amount of light passing through the lens, compensation in exposure must be made. With cameras that have TTL meters this will be done automatically, but for manually operated cameras this must be taken into account before the final exposure is made. This is quite easy as each filter comes with a number known as a filter factor which indicates the amount of compensation required for each exposure. For instance a filter factor of 1 requires one stop increase in exposure.

● TOP RIGHT In this picture no filter was used. Although the image is correctly exposed it has a slightly blue cast which makes it look rather cold. The sky lacks definition and appears flat.

● TOP, FAR RIGHT By adding an 81A filter the blue cast has been reduced, the picture appears warmer and the contrast between the different tones is increased.

● BOTTOM RIGHT In this picture an 81EF filter was used to eradicate the blueness of the overall picture. The grass and tree are well defined and the clouds and sky have body.

● BOTTOM, FAR RIGHT As well as using an 81EF filter, a neutral density graduated filter has been added. This filter allows two differing areas of brightness to be brought into line with one another. In this case the hill and background required an exposure of ¹/₁₂₅ second at f8, but the sky only needed an exposure of ¹/₁₂₅ at f11. The graduated filter brings both areas into line so that the sky is well defined yet the land area is not underexposed.

● RIGHT Here a polarizing filter has been used. This has made the blue sky darker and the wispy white clouds stand out with great clarity. If this filter is used with an SLR camera the effect can be seen in the viewfinder as the filter is rotated.

LANDSCAPES: GENERAL COMPOSITION

The main subject matter of photographs taken while travelling will probably be landscapes. In landscape photography it is very important to take care with composition to avoid producing dull shots, for example of a lot of sky with only a thin strip of land. A commonplace image can be transformed very simply by paying attention to shadow, colour and detail, all of which are paramount in producing good landscape shots.

● LEFT This grouping of trees is common around the River Po in northern Italy. The planting arrangement is exaggerated by going in close using a wide angle lens so that the long lines between the rows form a focal point for the composition. The evening light helps to create a pleasant atmosphere.

● ABOVE Give some thought to which lens to use when composing a landscape shot: it is one of the most important factors in a successful composition. By using a 200 mm telephoto lens this picture has been framed without any sky. The eye is drawn to the slightly pink terrain of the foreground while the grey rock of the canyon forms the background. The long lens has compressed the shot, further emphasizing the foreground. The trees in the foreground look like tiny bushes and this gives an indication of the scale of the canyon.

● LEFT AND BELOW Although these two shots were taken very close to each other, one is a far better composition than the other. In the upright picture the road and tree balance one another, drawing the eye to the centre. The tree is a bold dominant feature; the way the narrow road converges adds a sense of curiosity – what lies beyond? In the horizontal picture the tree appears to lose its dominance and the expanse of fields on either side diminishes the power of the converging sides of the road. It is clear that the smallest adjustment can make a considerable difference to the overall composition.

VARYING A LANDSCAPE SHOT

- Rotate the camera slightly to one side; this may cut out unwanted scenery or bring in an added point of interest.

- Move the camera from a horizontal to a vertical position; sometimes the smallest of movements which does not even involve moving your feet can have a dramatic effect.

- Try isolating a portion of the landscape against a backdrop from a different part of the image; this can emphasize scale or make a coloured field, for example, stand out from surrounding pastures.

- Notice the position of any trees; a single isolated tree or a group of trees apart from a wood or forest can be used as a device for leading the eye into the scene. Tractor furrows or a meandering stream or river have a similar effect.

- An object in one corner of the picture adds to the composition; be careful that there is enough variety in a sequence of shots – do not always place an object in the same corner or the series begins to look dull.

Often the view that looks most spectacular to your eyes does not come out nearly so well on film. This is not necessarily because of any technical fault: it may be just that the wrong viewpoint was chosen when pressing the shutter. All the time you look at anything, your eyes are editing the scene and suppressing uninteresting details. In contrast, the camera records just what is in front of it, and unless you have taken care to exclude things you do not want, they will appear on the print.

In many cases the picture could be improved beyond recognition by moving a short distance. The basic viewpoint may be fine, but perhaps a higher or lower viewpoint is needed; try standing on a step, or crouching down. It is worth taking time to explore a variety of viewpoints. Even when you have taken your shot and are walking away you may suddenly see a better shot. If you do, take it. After all, film is the least expensive component in photography. You may never return to that place, or the light may never be the same again – so do not worry about using up another couple of frames.

PARALLAX ERROR

One common reason for not getting the picture wanted is parallax error. A camera with a separate viewfinder for the lens – that is, most cameras except single lens reflex cameras – gives a slight difference in framing between what you see and the picture you take. This makes no noticeable difference when photographing a distant object or a landscape, but the closer you go in, the greater the error. If the landscape shot has a foreground you will certainly have to allow for parallax. If you do not, a detail you expect to be in your photograph may simply not appear, and vice versa.

● BELOW, LEFT AND RIGHT From looking at the background of the buildings and cliffs it is clear that both these pictures were taken from almost the same place. But the foregrounds are quite different. This shows the effect that altering the viewpoint slightly can have on the finished picture. Although both compositions work well, the one on the LEFT is taken from a better viewpoint in relation to the sun.

● RIGHT A central viewpoint from a bridge over both the railway track and the canal has created an interesting composition. A fairly slow shutter speed of ¹⁄₆₀ of a second was used. This has made the express train slightly blurred. But instead of being a fault, it adds an air of movement and speed. In contrast the canal looks calm and tranquil, a bygone and slower mode of transport. The viewpoint contributes greatly to the juxtaposition.

● BELOW Taking this shot from a viewpoint some way up the bank of the lake has brought the pavilion on the far side into clear view. A view from near the water's edge would have made the bridge in the middle distance cut into the pavilion, spoiling the composition.

LANDSCAPES: THE WEATHER

There is no such thing as perfect weather for photography. Of course, photographing people on a beach holiday in the pouring rain may present a few difficulties, but many inclement weather situations are in fact the basis for original and dramatic photographs. Overcast skies can be used to advantage and reveal more about the immediate environment than if the sun were shining on a clear day. Rain can be evocative, portraying isolation and stormy conditions. Wintry, and especially snow-covered views provide good, clear images; these are best shot in sunshine to obtain the best view of the shadows cast on crisp snow – an effect which is lost if the sky is heavy.

Predicting where light will fall is important; try to look at a map to gauge where the sun will shine strongly, and rise and set. Make sure the camera is in position at the right time to get the full effect of the quality of light required, particularly if unusual weather conditions produce dramatic cloud formations.

CAMERA CARE IN EXTREME CONDITIONS

If the weather is very cold the shutter on the camera may freeze and valuable picture opportunities may be lost. Extreme heat can ruin film so keep it wrapped in aluminium foil as this will keep it a little cooler. As big a lens hood as possible may help to shield the lens from the rain; beware of cutting off the corners, or 'vignetting' the picture. Do not let weather conditions prevent photography – be prepared to have a go: the results could be surprising!

• LEFT Mist and fog should not be a deterrent to photographers. This almost monochromatic picture has a strange eerie quality to it. Is the boat perhaps drifting and abandoned? Hazy air can add an enigmatic quality to shots.

• ABOVE AND RIGHT Snow creates wonderful picture possibilities. Take care not to underexpose: there is so much reflected light that exposure meters may read the conditions as being much brighter than they are. Try waiting for different light on snowscenes. Here the picture with the sun shining brightly, RIGHT, certainly enhances the overall effect.

• ABOVE Even in the rain dramatic pictures can be taken. This storm over the Atlantic illustrates the qualities of cold and isolation. A slow shutter speed can help to emphasize the driving rain.

• LEFT Prior calculation of where the sun is going to set means that full advantage can be taken of warm evening light, as here where the sun falls on the shapes of the clouds. The same shot taken earlier in the day would have lacked such intensity, warmth and atmosphere.

• LEFT The heavy rain cloud hanging over the limestone pavement illustrates perfectly the visual effect overcast weather can produce. Here it is particularly apt as the cloud hangs over rock which has been eroded by rainfall over the centuries, so the image has a double purpose, it is visually pleasing as well as instructive.

LANDSCAPES: TIME OF DAY

Throughout the day the sun constantly changes position. In photographic terms this movement is more than one from east to west: any change in the sun will produce a different effect on any landscape. In the early morning and evening the sun will be quite low; the shadows it casts will be long and dramatic. In winter the sun will be lower still and these shadows will be even more exaggerated. At midday the sun will be high and the shadows cast will be shorter. In some cases this can lead to flat and featureless shots, so care must be taken at this time of day.

The other factor to consider is that the light cast by the sun in the early morning and late afternoon will have a warmer tone than that of midday light, so pictures taken at these times will appear redder or more orange than those taken in the middle of the day. It is well worth making the effort to get up early, before the sun rises, to be in position to capture the quality of light as dawn breaks. A little research beforehand will show where the sun will be and what it will fall on, depending on the time of year. Early and late rays of sunlight can illuminate an isolated area of a landscape in much the same way as a giant spotlight trained on the scene.

● ABOVE LEFT This shot was taken at mid-morning, yet there is enough of an angle in the light from the sun to create shadow detail. The well-defined clouds have broken up what could have been a bland sky so that the general result has equal focus and visual impact in all areas.

● ABOVE RIGHT The early evening sun was very low on the horizon when this picture was taken. It has just started to tinge the clouds with red and darken the golden sand. By using a wide aperture, a fast enough shutter speed could be used to capture the gently breaking waves.

● RIGHT AND BELOW RIGHT These two pictures were taken from the same viewpoint, the one BELOW after the sun had set. The sky is bathed in a dramatic red-orange light. In contrast the shot taken in the morning, on the RIGHT, had the sun behind the camera and the quality of light is much cooler. A polarizing filter was used to enhance the colour of the sea.

● LEFT This picture was taken just after the sun has risen and the quality of light is very warm, casting a golden reflection on the River Thames. The early morning mist has diffused the sun and gently bathed the scene with a sense of calm. A little prior research meant that the picture was taken at exactly the time the sun appeared between the dome of St Paul's Cathedral and the National Westminster Bank Tower. If the shot had been taken two months earlier, the sun would have appeared to the right of the tower; four months later it would have been to the left of the cathedral dome.

PEOPLE IN LANDSCAPES

Landscape photography is often enhanced by the inclusion of a human figure. This technique of combining people with landscapes can be used to illustrate a particular activity in a certain area, or to show the type of landscape a person may work or live in. Human figures add scale to a particular feature of a landscape, such as a large rock or the height of a tree. Showing a person isolated within a landscape is an effective way of showing the desolate or lonely aspect of a region. On overcast days a person can help to enliven an otherwise dull situation. If the person is working try to let them continue with the task already started. Reassure the subject that he or she is a welcome part of the shot – many people assume that they are in the way and try to move out of the picture.

On a walking holiday, for instance, it might be better if your companions were seen coming through a gate or along a path while the camera is positioned on higher ground than the people to be included; but also remember not to let your shadow creep into the picture. In the early morning or late afternoon shadows will be well defined and long. If people are to feature in the foreground of a picture make sure that they do not block out an important point of interest in the middle or background. On the other hand, if there is something unsightly in the background the inclusion of a person can help conceal the object.

● RIGHT The shepherd in the foreground helps to create a sense of space between himself and his village. He also diverts the eye away from the overcast weather. Local people are often very pleased to be in photographs; do not be afraid to ask them to pose.

● ABOVE The man has been included in this picture to give a sense of scale; without him it would be almost impossible to tell accurately how high the waterfall is. Consider the picture without the man: as well as losing the sense of scale, the composition would be entirely different without the added point of interest which makes an intriguing juxtaposition to the waterfall.

● LEFT This shot was taken in the early morning light. The warm tones of the sun highlight every feature of the man's face while the cliffs behind provide both an interesting backdrop and a sense of location. This type of light would be too harsh for some people, and it may be better to wait for the position of the sun to move or to move the person into a shaded area.

● BELOW This shot was taken in winter; the people standing by the seashore add a clear sense of the desolation of the beach at this time of year, yet in contrast the setting sun bathes the sky and surrounding landscape with a warm glow.

BLACK AND WHITE LANDSCAPES

Often a black and white photograph of a landscape or seascape can be far more evocative and dramatic than one taken in colour.

One important thing to remember is that some detail, for instance in a cloudy sky, can become flat and grey if a filter is not used. To make white puffy clouds stand out against the sky use a yellow filter. For even greater drama use a red one, which will turn the sky very dark.

Provided there is detail on the negative, the sky can be 'burnt in' at printing stage. This means giving certain areas of a print more exposure ('printing them up') or less exposure ('holding them back') than the rest of the picture by partly masking the print under the darkroom enlarger.

Another advantage of black and white for print making is that there is a variety of paper grades to choose from. A print made on grade 1 paper will be soft, and one made on grade 3 much harder. The whole feel of a picture can be altered by choice of paper alone.

In colour photography there is contrast between different colours as well as different tones. The essence of a good black and white picture is its tonal range. This does not mean that there have to be extremes of white at one end and black at the other. That would be a high contrast print, and it might be interesting; but it is the subtlety of gradations of tone that make a rich print. Fine-grained film, 100 ISO or less, will give better shadow detail than faster film, and will allow far bigger enlargements to be made.

To see how good a black and white landscape can be, study the work of the late American photographer Ansel Adams whose studies are epitomized by their starkly contrasting tones.

● ABOVE Keeping the rooftops in the foreground has increased the feeling of depth in this picture. A medium telephoto lens, 150 mm, was used and this has very slightly compressed the picture, bringing the town on the other side of the river closer in.

● TOP LEFT This picture shows a good tonal range. The camera was fitted with a wide angle lens and pointed downward to emphasize the texture of the rock in the foreground. A neutral density graduated filter was used to retain detail in the sky, and this was further emphasized when the print was made.

● BOTTOM LEFT This high-key picture of sand dunes has an almost tactile quality. Keeping the tones to the lighter end of the range has enhanced the softness of the windswept sand and given the picture a feeling of peace. When working in conditions like these be careful that sand does not get into equipment.

● LEFT Filters can make a dramatic difference to black and white photographs, as this shot shows. A red filter has turned the sky very dark. For a less extreme effect, a yellow filter will help to retain detail of white clouds.

SEASCAPES

Special care must be taken when photographing seascapes as misleading exposure meter readings can occur. In an environment with so many reflective surfaces the meter can be fooled into measuring the scene as brighter than it is. This can lead to underexposure and disappointing results. To overcome this problem take a meter reading close up of some mid-tone detail.

If the camera is one with built-in autoexposure but no manual override, first decide on the composition. Then point the camera to an area of mid-tone detail such as grey rock. Depress the shutter release button half-way; this will activate the meter and the camera will record the reading. Keeping the shutter depressed in this position, move the camera back to the scene of the original composition. Now gently depress the shutter release button fully and take the picture. To take a similar picture from a slightly different viewpoint, you will have to repeat the process for each shot.

Some cameras with a built-in autoexposure meter have a special mark on the shutter ring labelled AEL, or autoexposure lock, for taking readings like this. Its action is similar to semi-depressing the shutter release button.

● LEFT Movement in the sea at the Giants' Causeway in Northern Ireland is captured and emphasized by a slow shutter speed, to make it look as if the sea is really pounding at the unusual hexagonal rocks that are a famous landmark in this area. The rocks are lit by warm light as sunset approaches, and the strong shadows bring out these strange forms.

● BELOW This picture was taken as a hurricane approached; in high winds it is important to hold the camera steady, perhaps bracing it on a firm surface such as a rock or low wall if you do not have a tripod. Even at relatively fast shutter speeds, such as $\frac{1}{125}$ second, camera shake will lead to blurred pictures.

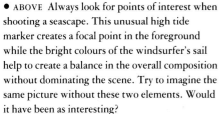

● ABOVE Always look for points of interest when shooting a seascape. This unusual high tide marker creates a focal point in the foreground while the bright colours of the windsurfer's sail help to create a balance in the overall composition without dominating the scene. Try to imagine the same picture without these two elements. Would it have been as interesting?

● BELOW The addition of a polarizing filter for this shot gives the sea a translucent quality. In order to check the effect of a polarizing filter when using an SLR camera, rotate the filter while looking through the viewfinder, until the desired effect has been achieved.

SPECIAL EQUIPMENT FOR SEASCAPE SHOTS

1 A lens hood – this should be fitted at all times, whether or not beside the sea, but is particularly important in cutting down any unwanted reflections which may flare on the lens.

2 A polarizing filter – this makes the blue colours of the sky much richer and enhances the clarity of any small white clouds. The filter will also change the reflective nature of the surface of the sea.

Lakes, rivers, streams or canals offer an entirely different variety of photographic opportunities from those found by the sea and in coastal regions. The surrounding areas are often reflected in the surface of the water, adding an extra dimension to the shot and reproducing what is often the most spectacular scenery twice over.

The same problems of measuring exposure encountered when taking seascapes also apply to pictures of large stretches of fresh or inland water; the exposure metering system may judge light as being brighter than it is because of the light coming from the expanse of reflective water. As with sea shots, compensation must be made for this in order to avoid underexposure and ruined pictures.

Take care when choosing a viewpoint for water photography. Make sure the surface, especially of rivers or canals, is free of factory effluent, waste products and debris, unless this is the detail to be highlighted.

● LEFT If a shot is taken very early in the morning the water surface is often quite still. This creates a perfect mirroring medium. The inclusion of the single cloud adds depth to the image as well as providing an extra point of interest, drawing the eye upwards as well as to the reflection in the water.

● RIGHT Colour and detail are not always easy to find in the composition of a water shot. Here the canal boats add bright spots of colour in what would otherwise be a rather dull stretch of water. The trees help block out unwanted buildings and provide a neat frame for the picture.

● LEFT This shot was taken from a rock set slightly out from the bank. The exposure used here was calculated to give maximum depth of field and the slowest possible shutter speed. This means that the rock in the foreground is very sharp while the water is blurred, emphasizing the speed at which the river is flowing.

● BELOW Choice of viewpoint is always of paramount importance when photographing water, especially where reflection is included. Here the dramatic picture of the reflected snow-capped mountain is altered by the plants growing beneath the water. Make sure there are no unwanted intrusions in the final shot.

SHOOTING STILL WATER

Water is usually at its stillest very early in the morning before the wind, if there is any, has begun to blow. If the surface of the water is completely still, the surrounding scenery reflected in it can produce a striking mirror image. Try mounting the final prints vertically instead of in the conventional horizontal fashion. At first glance the picture will be a striking abstract image and many unusual and often amusing effects can be produced by a little experimentation with presentation angles.

SKIES

According to the time of year, the ever-changing light, weather conditions, cloud formations and seasonal changes provide an endless range of photographic opportunities when taking pictures of the sky. Although sunsets are a favourite subject for many photographers, not all sky shots need be taken at dusk, and in fact many of the most effective shots are captured at different times of the day.

The essential point to remember when photographing skies is to judge the exposure so that the important details, such as clouds, are recorded. A polarizing filter will help to darken the sky while retaining the detail if the shot is of a blue sky with puffy white clouds. A neutral density graduated filter could be used to similar effect or, for real drama, combined with the polarizing filter. As well as the neutral density graduated filter, a graduated colour filter such as a tobacco graduated filter can be added. This will turn the sky a sepia colour while retaining the natural colour of the land.

When photographing an area you know well, try to be in position early to take advantage of the changing light patterns and the different effects this has on the sky.

When shooting at sunset be prepared to work rapidly as the sun sets very quickly. Also be on the lookout for the changing colour of the sky. Once the sun has set the sky can deepen in colour considerably. At sunset watch for light playing on clouds; an aura of light from these will look far more dramatic than a clear sky. As exposures will be quite long at this time of day a tripod is essential, and a cable release preferable.

● BELOW Here there is an almost perfect mirror image of the sky captured in the surface of the sea. It is best to take this kind of picture when the water is very calm. Watch out for unsightly objects or rubbish floating in the foreground.

● ABOVE This picture was taken just before the sun sank beneath the horizon and its light bathes the few clouds that remain in a golden aura. At this time of day a tripod is essential as the exposure required will be quite long.

REFLECTED SKIES

Skies that reflect into water, for example, make very good subjects. Either try to photograph the water when the air is completely still so that a perfect mirror image is achieved, or isolate a small area of water such as a puddle or pond to create foreground interest.

● LEFT By using a medium neutral density graduated filter all the detail of the clouds has been retained. A wide angle lens combined with a low viewpoint has emphasized the sky and it dominates the picture.

● RIGHT This shot was taken just before sunset. By using the small amount of water in the foreground interest is focused on the sky and the composition greatly enhanced. The backlighting on the ripples of the wet sand has added texture. In a situation like this carefully consider the reflective surface from various positions to obtain the best viewpoint.

REFLECTIONS

Reflected images, whether in buildings, water or glass, can make intriguing pictures. The majority of these can be made to look very abstract and as such can be very rewarding photographs. Shop windows, car body work, modern buildings: a close look at any of these will yield a surprising number of opportunities. Examine the materials buildings are constructed from; different types of glass will reflect in a variety of ways, for example. The many panes in an older window, for instance, will provide a multiple-image reflection. The many angles of a modern glass building mean that the image can be photographed reflected into itself. As well as creating fascinating shots of modern architecture the eye is led into a visual conundrum. Try having several prints made of such images and have half of them reversed. When they are mounted together the effect can be quite startling and a whole new range of creative possibilities opens up. This effect works equally well in black and white as well as colour.

Rain, or rather the puddles it creates, also offers many opportunities for interesting reflections. A wet road, too, can provide a strong reflective surface, but beware of flare.

● RIGHT Well-known landmarks can look refreshingly different when photographed reflected in another surface. Always be on the look-out for modern buildings with mirror glass which, depending on the angles, will reflect itself or typical aspects of a city in a new way. Here the familiar London bus is blurred but quite recognizable although it has taken on an abstract quality.

• ABOVE A multiplicity of reflections and neon light make this picture into a strong graphic image. This shot was taken at dusk; the same scene in daylight lacked impact. Always think about the surrounding lighting: the bright colours of neon lights, especially those in signs which are constantly changing, can give extraordinary results reflected in wet surfaces.

• TOP RIGHT This picture of the Rio Grande illustrates just how perfect some mirror images can be. If viewed on its side it takes on a completely different dimension. Many images lend themselves to this treatment and it is worth experimenting with aspects of presentation for a varied effect.

• BOTTOM RIGHT This shot was taken into a shop window in Chinatown, Los Angeles. At first the images are confusing as it is not immediately obvious what is reflected in which surface. The green flag with the strong Chinese lettering is the backdrop to the shop window, and the street scene is reflected into the window. Optical illusions of this type arouse curiosity as well as providing unique photographic images.

• ABOVE This shot is a combination of reflected neon light, glass and steel which has several visual layers to it. By choosing the viewpoint with care, a strong geometrical composition is created.

AUTUMN

Each season has its unique characteristics but autumn provides the photographer with a range of colours that lend themselves immediately to composition. Of all the seasons it is the one that lasts the shortest. Just when a tree is at its peak a strong gust of wind can blow off most of its leaves leaving it stark and bare. Even without wind a tree will take a little over two weeks to shed its leaves so it is important to seize the opportunity quickly for photographing these tremendous colours. As well as photographing large swathes of broad-leafed trees try to look for spots of isolated colour to provide contrast. These might be provided by a lone tree set in a landscape or a single leaf blown onto the ground.

Experiment by being aware of situations from different angles. Looking up towards a blue sky can make a wonderful backdrop to golden leaves, while the use of a wide angle lens in a forest can, from a low viewpoint, make trees appear to soar skyward.

● LEFT It is not only trees and leaves that present an image of autumn: these windfall apples show what can be found by the alert photographer. Always be on the lookout for the unexpected.

● BELOW A low viewpoint is used to its full advantage here. The slender tree trunks soar skyward and their golden leaves form a colourful canopy. There is just enough light filtering through onto the foliage below to form some interesting patterns and keep the exposure even.

PHOTOGRAPHING AUTUMN LEAVES

● Try to place leaves together and examine the contrasts in their colours, shapes and sizes.

● Consider what the leaves might look like backlit.

● When photographing leaves in close-up so that the detail of the veins as well as the colour becomes a vital part of the image, extension rings or bellows will probably be necessary.

● When backlighting leaves or photographing from very close up, the leaf must be kept still. Some sort of windbreak may be needed; alternatively a modest lighting set-up can be erected indoors and the leaves arranged there. Whichever method is used, always watch out for large uninteresting shadows; these may not be very noticeable at first, but once photographed in close-up a small area may look ugly if one leaf casts a long shadow onto another.

● FAR LEFT Autumn is a rapidly changing season and the photographer needs to be aware of this to take full advantage of the range of shots available. A few days before this shot was taken these ferns were green. Now, the early morning light has intensified their deep rust colour. The tree in the foreground leads the eye into the picture and helps break up an almost entirely blue sky.

● ABOVE Autumn leaves provide very good detail for close-up shots. These were photographed against the sky. If a slow shutter speed is used wind may be a problem unless the subject is shielded.

PEOPLE

If you study travel photographs you will be surprised at how often you can recognize the country, even a particular city, by looking at the people in the shots. This may be something as obvious as a shot of a guard outside Buckingham Palace or a portrait of someone in front of the Eiffel Tower. But other, more ordinary forms of dress can also convey location – especially when combined with architecture.

Thanks not only to our own travels but also to television, newspapers and magazines, many parts of the world are now more familiar. Photographs which in the past would have been fascinating glimpses of exotic places are in danger of becoming mere clichés, but adding people to these views can lift them out of the ordinary.

Most local people do not mind having their photographs taken and some, such as uniformed guards, positively expect it. In all these pictures the people were unknown to the photographer, but in three of them it is clear that they were well aware of being the main focus of interest.

Always look out for the unexpected detail that gives the key to the location. It could be a sign on a door or a detail of a building, even something as mundane as an advertising hoarding. Clothing, as well as the overall lighting of the picture, gives a good idea of the climate of a place.

Think about viewpoint when taking pictures like these. It may be worthwhile to crouch down and take the shot from below. It will make people look more dominant than if you are looking down on them. Consider also whether it is best to have them in the centre of the frame or to one side. In the latter case, if you are using autofocus and your camera has an autoexposure lock, first point the camera at the people, semi-depress the shutter release and hold it down to lock the setting, then move the camera to the desired position and take your shot.

● ABOVE By restricting the depth of field, the buildings in the background have been put out of focus very slightly. This has helped emphasize the guard's vivid red uniform and the fine detail on his helmet so that he becomes the focal point.

● ABOVE The girl is small, but a low viewpoint has made her the centre of interest. Always think carefully about the angle from which you take your portraits. The slightest change can alter the emphasis.

● LEFT These people in Orvieto in Italy made a diverse group. Shots like this one can be used in a series of pictures of an area to lend it human interest.

● LEFT The beer truck made an interesting background. Always be aware of unusual possibilities. The man was a complete stranger, but he was perfectly happy to be photographed. His clothing and the background positively shout 'America!'

When travelling, good shots of people in their working environment can complement scenic pictures and add an extra dimension to a record of a journey. These pictures will often provide a more intimate insight into places visited and show what is special about a particular area. They can be displayed in an album beside pictures of landscapes, buildings and family. Shots of factories or farms which offer tours, waiters serving in a favourite restaurant, or a craft centre with unusual items – these may all capture the essence of the holiday or trip and serve as a useful reference later on.

If the work that people are engaged in is very detailed, try to get in close so you can see what they are doing. Remember not to get in their way and so become a nuisance or they may refuse to allow the picture to be taken.

If you are indoors and the light is low flash may be needed. Try to bounce it off the ceiling or diffuse it. Nothing is worse than a harsh blast of strong flashlight that burns out the foreground but leaves the background dark and murky. Pay attention to the background, too; does it add something to the shot? Does it provide any information about the work being done, or is it a useful plain backdrop?

● RIGHT The waiters and waitresses in this café in New Orleans are relaxing while off duty. This type of shot shows not only people in their work environment but also helps to build up an overall picture of life in a particular town or city. Try to think ahead and decide which aspects of a trip will be the most memorable and descriptive.

● BELOW These men work in the malting room of a whisky distillery on the Orkney Islands of Scotland. By including their work implements in the picture a clear image of their job is captured as well as adding an air of spontaneous activity. The same implements also served as convenient resting posts while the men steadied themselves during the long exposure.

● BELOW Always look around to examine what props are available; these are usually part of the person's work and add extra visual interest to the picture as well as providing information about the job itself. If the people to be featured in the shot seem shy, start by taking pictures of the surroundings so that they become used to a photographer's presence. Talk to them about their work. If they sense genuine interest they will soon gain confidence and appear naturally relaxed in the picture.

● LEFT This man is one of the few professional lute makers in existence. The work is very delicate and slow; one slip of a chisel and the whole instrument could be ruined. This shot was taken by a window using the available daylight that is filtering through. The intensity of the work is reflected in his expression. A 100 mm lens was used to afford a clear view of what he was doing while still keeping some distance from him.

LOCAL PEOPLE

People will add colour to travel pictures, especially when featured in shots presented alongside others concentrating on landscape, architecture or the sea. A series of pictures of the people of a locality can form a portrait of life in that region. To catch the spirit of local activities, go in close so that people are related to their work or environment.

When photographing strangers politeness is the key. If people are approached in a friendly and reassuring way only the most recalcitrant will object to being photographed. Remember, though, that in some parts of the world it is inadvisable to photograph people – or even to make drawings of them. In some cultures there is a belief that if people are photographed their soul is removed. However strange such an opinion may seem it is important to respect it. Remonstrating with people will only make matters worse. It would be far more productive to find someone in authority and use your best diplomatic skills to get them to reassure and persuade your subjects to give their assent. In most cases such an approach, aided perhaps by a small gift, will win the day. A very effective method is to offer them a Polaroid portrait.

● BELOW Being quick to spot a good shot and seize the moment is the essence of a good travel shot. This grape grower was seen driving his tractor laden with grapes down a country lane. He agreed to be photographed, and a series of portraits was taken in the late afternoon sun.

● RIGHT Using a wide angle lens together with a small aperture has given good depth of field. This means that the spices are in focus as well as the two stall holders. The vivid colours of the spices create strong foreground interest and lead the eye into the picture.

● RIGHT Careful selection of colour will say much about the climate of a locality. It does not always have to be vivid; here the colours are muted but give a feeling of warmth. This shepherd was spotted by chance on a drive through a remote part of Sicily. Although his sheep were giving him and his dog problems he readily agreed to be photographed. His clothes convey the feeling of someone who works out of doors, and his hat indicates that the climate is hot, protecting him from the strong sunlight. Such ingredients in photographs put across a sense of place.

● LEFT Close cropping of these soldiers emphasizes their rich uniforms, and the gold of the gates behind them forms an effective backdrop. As events like this happen on a daily basis in most capital cities, you will have many opportunities to shoot local ceremonies.

Buildings present the photographer with an inexhaustible supply of imagery. The most important part of photographing any building is the general composition. The weather can be perfect, the exposure correct and the time of day just right, but a badly-framed picture will ruin everything. Here, equipment can be a great help:

● a telephoto lens will not only bring closer a distant building but also, depending on the power of the lens, compress the overall view and so reduce the illusion of space between the main building in the shot and those that may be behind or in front of it.

● a wide angle lens allows a close-up shot with an exaggerated perspective. A tall building such as a skyscraper can appear even taller if the camera is pointed upwards because the verticals will converge.

● a shift lens allows the photographer to avoid converging verticals in situations where these are not wanted as part of the shot. A shift lens alters the axis of view without the need to move the camera, yet allows movement of the lens in relationship to the film plane.

Choosing the correct viewpoint is a vital ingredient for general composition. Position the camera so that there are no unwanted objects within the frame. This may mean simply moving a short distance or using a different lens. If the camera is fitted with a zoom lens all that may be needed is a small adjustment in its focal length.

● ABOVE A telephoto lens was used for this shot of an isolated Scottish house; the top of the mountains that form the backdrop was deliberately cropped out. By composing a picture in this way the isolation of the subject is emphasized and becomes a particular point of focal interest.

● LEFT A small telephoto lens of 100 mm was used for this shot. This slightly compresses the buildings making the composition very tight. Ensure that any vehicles or other unwanted intrusions have been moved before taking the shot, or try to stand in a position where they would be cropped out of the frame.

● ABOVE The railings around the church form a frame for this picture and produce a pleasing composition. Although a wide angle lens was used the viewpoint was close enough to prevent the church receding too far into the distance. The puffy white clouds help to break up the blue sky and enhance the composition, adding another visual element.

● ABOVE By waiting until dusk a certain quality of light is captured; here the tower is bathed in a warm glow. The reflection of the building in the water helps to give a greater illusion of height. The use of a shift lens means that there are no converging verticals, yet the whole building still fits the frame. Remember to ensure that when photographing modern buildings light is not reflected off their exterior surfaces and into the camera lens.

BUILDINGS: EXTERIORS

Sometimes it seems enough to simply stand in front of a great building, point the camera and press the shutter, especially if the building is so famous that there does not seem to be anything to add. In many cases this may be true, but if everyone followed this path the results would be repetitive and tedious. There are always new ways of representing a familiar object: unusual angles, different lighting conditions, a section of an exterior. All these elements can enhance any photograph of a building.

ATMOSPHERIC DETAILS

- Time of day is an important consideration when photographing buildings. If, from a chosen viewpoint, the sun rises behind the building, this could result in a hazy image making the building look rather flat. If there is time, wait until the sun moves round, perhaps bathing the building in a warm afternoon light and creating strong shadow detail.

- Clouds can provide an added dimension. Sometimes even a radiantly blue sky will benefit from a few puffy white clouds above a building. Also, billowing storm clouds will add drama and perhaps a somewhat theatrical appearance to the shot.

● LEFT The New University in Moscow was photographed when the sun was at its highest and therefore illuminating the exterior evenly. A shift lens was used so that the full height of the tower could be included in the shot without needing to tilt the camera upwards. This would have caused converging verticals.

● LEFT Isolated in a mountain range, this white church stands out in a shaft of sunlight. This shot was taken after waiting for half an hour while a cloud obscured the sun; without the sunlight the scene was flat and uninteresting. It is always worth waiting for changes in the light to obtain a better photograph.

● BELOW By standing to one side of this street a rather ugly wall was cropped out. A medium telephoto lens, 135 mm, was used and has slightly compressed the buildings and brought closer the fields in the background. This has produced a tight composition with the emphasis on the row of housing without any unsightly distractions.

● ABOVE This shot was taken using a medium telephoto lens. The buildings in the foreground have been retained in the frame to enhance the cathedral of Siena as it stands majestically over them, dominating the skyline. The whole city is bathed in late afternoon light which adds warmth and enhances the predominantly terracotta hues of the buildings.

● ABOVE The white puffy clouds, enhanced by a polarizing filter, hang gently over these adobe buildings at Taos, New Mexico, and help to provide extra detail. They also break up the otherwise somewhat monochromatic shot.

SHOOTING VERTICALS

Different lenses can completely alter the perspective of a building. Pointing the camera upwards, at a skyscraper for instance, will make the verticals converge. This can add greatly to the dynamic qualities of the image.

On the other hand, another building could be shown with converging verticals and might look distorted, seeming to be in danger of toppling over. Every building composition should be assessed individually.

A telephoto lens can be used to photograph a building from a distance. The building can be brought closer and the foreground compressed. This will give the impression of increased grandeur to the main building in the shot.

For more specialist photography of very tall buildings a shift lens can be used. This allows a building to be photographed so that its vertical lines remain upright without needing to tilt the camera upwards. This would create converging verticals.

● ABOVE This picture of a skyscraper shows the extreme effect of converging verticals. By pointing the camera upwards the height of the building has been exaggerated and its sides appear to meet at a point in the sky. A wide angle lens has helped to emphasize this effect.

BUILDINGS: INTERIORS

One of the main points to consider before photographing the interior of a building is the amount of light available. In the majority of cases this is very little compared to that available outdoors. Our eyes are adept at adjusting to different light conditions, so adept that we soon cease to notice that certain conditions are in fact rather dull. With film, however, even relatively fast film, there is no such natural adjustment. The only way to record a usable image is to increase the exposure or to light the interior artificially by using flash.

Many cameras have built-in flash or a flash attachment connected to the hot shoe of the camera or to a bracket on one side of the camera body. However, even with the most powerful of these flash units there still may not be enough light to illuminate the interiors of very large and grand buildings. Even where a fast film is used with available light the result is very grainy and much of the shadow detail will be lost. A far better solution is to mount the camera on a tripod and use a long exposure. Of the pictures shown on this page none was shot on film faster than 64 ISO, and in only one picture was flash used as well.

Inside great monuments crowded with visitors some extra thought should be given to viewpoint so that the shot will not include other people. In some monuments tripods are not permitted; in this case use a monopod or find a suitable surface, such as a pew, floor, table or window sill, on which to rest the camera.

● ABOVE This interior was shot entirely in natural light. The blinds were angled to let in as much sun as possible while at the same time using them as a creative tool to cast interesting shadows. The result is a thoroughly modern interior bathed in bright sunlight.

● LEFT In this shot the window is illuminated by the daylight outside. This was not powerful enough to illuminate the walls inside without burning out the detail of the stained glass. By balancing the exposure of the flash on the walls with the light coming in through the window an even exposure was achieved.

● RIGHT By using a fisheye lens, an unusual angle of the ceiling of Westminster Abbey has been achieved. Even though the Abbey was opened to the public, tilting the camera upwards means that people have been cropped out. The day was overcast so there are no strong shadows on the sides of the buildings. This made the exposure relatively even, although long, and no other lighting was required.

● RIGHT Flash is forbidden in the Long Room in the Old Library of Trinity College, Dublin, so available light was used. The shot was taken from the balcony to add a feeling of greater depth. If the shot had been taken from ground level the camera would have to have been tilted upwards and this would have led to converging verticals, giving the impression that the room was leaning inwards.

Buildings provide many opportunities for the photographer to create exciting and, in many ways, unusual images of scenes that are always present but which the majority of people pass by without noticing. Sometimes it is not always possible or indeed beneficial to include a building in its entirety in a single photograph. In some cases the building may be quite dull and it is only by isolating a small section of carving or ceramics, for instance, that a strong shot will be obtained.

The time of day can play an important part in photographing details. When the sun is low or at an acute angle to the subject strong shadows will be created. This can enhance the graphic qualities and result in unusual, if not abstract, images.

It will be rare that an interesting angle cannot be found for even the most mundane building, and in the majority of cases what makes a photograph 'good' is the amount of time the photographer has spent looking for an unusual angle, going in close on detail and framing the picture to hide or crop unwanted intrusions. In certain cases close up shots of architectural detail may, over a period of time, provide a series of pictures that could be used together or to form a collection of individual themes or styles. With interior details precise framing can be important and it would be beneficial to use a tripod. This is not just in instances where there will probably be less light and so longer exposures will be necessary, but also in situations where symmetry is a key element, for example with a ceiling. Nothing is worse than seeing a final image where care has been taken with exposure and general composition but where one of four pillars, for example, is not quite square. With a tripod this 'squaring up' can be achieved with a greater degree of precision than can be expected with a hand-held camera.

● ABOVE It was impossible to fit the whole of Florence cathedral into a single shot. Also there were all the unsightly aspects of mass tourism that seemed at odds with this majestic building. By concentrating on one section and pointing the camera up above ground level the shot shows the uninterrupted beauty of the stone work.

● LEFT The hallway of the old *Daily Express* newspaper building in London's Fleet Street is one of the capital's greatest Art Deco interiors. Although the hallway is still intact many such interiors have been lost forever and photographs remain the only historical document of their existence. Needless to say these photographs could be very valuable in the years to come. To show the detail of this metallic mural it was lit from one side. If the light had been directly in front the picture would have looked flat and 'hot spots' would inevitably have appeared.

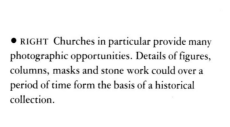

• ABOVE By going in close on these New York fire escapes and taking advantage of the low afternoon winter sun, a strong graphic image has been created. If the lower part of the building had been included the result would have been less abstract and therefore less dramatic.

• ABOVE The ground floor of this building had been converted into the most mundane offices with uninspiring furniture. The ceiling, in contrast, had been preserved and by choosing the viewpoint with precision and mounting the camera on a tripod a perfectly symmetrical image was achieved.

• RIGHT Churches in particular provide many photographic opportunities. Details of figures, columns, masks and stone work could over a period of time form the basis of a historical collection.

BUILDINGS AT NIGHT

Buildings seen at night can often be far more evocative of a cityscape than they appear to be in daylight hours. Some cities, such as New York, literally throb at night and are lit for the great part by garish neon light which looks strangely fitting.

The best time to take modern cityscape shots is about half an hour after sunset when the sky takes on a deep blue hue, which is far more attractive as a backdrop than a completely black sky. This quality of light lasts for a very short time, usually only 10–15 minutes. If you are prepared, such a length of time will be adequate, except of course that it will only provide perhaps one or two shots an evening. Because the light is low, exposures will be long and a tripod will be essential in most cases.

MAKING USE OF ADDITIONAL LIGHTS

- If the composition of the building includes a street the head- and tail-lights of passing cars can be an added ingredient. By using a slow shutter speed the lights will appear as trails of light snaking through the man-made canyons of the city.

- Be careful to avoid flare from external lighting such as street lamps. Sometimes a standard lens hood will be inadequate and a shield may need to be improvised from a piece of card, a book or a map, for instance; alternatively, shift position to stand between the camera and the light.

● ABOVE This shot was taken at the premium twilight hour. The camera viewpoint looks upwards. This has caused the two skyscrapers to converge but this has the effect of exaggerating their height and adding an impression of enclosure within the city.

The bus fills the bottom of the frame horizontally and reinforces the sense of movement. The thin side windows of the bus, turned green as they are lit by the fluorescent tubes, add to the theme of nightime and its artificial lighting in the city.

● BELOW This picture was taken when the sky was quite dark. As the building is well illuminated on the outside and fills most of the frame, the blackness of the sky forms a contrasting backdrop without being overpowering or dull.

● BELOW The main shot of the Coliseum in Rome strikes a perfect balance between the illumination of the stone of the building and the colour of the twilight sky. The trails of the head- and tail-lights of the traffic help to fill the void created by the road. The other shot, INSET, taken from the same viewpoint, shows the effect of inadequate lens shading as the flare from a street light has flawed the picture.

FLORA

Plants provide good material for the photographer. It is worth considering not only exotic plants but also more commonplace varieties. Apart from colour, texture plays an important part in a striking image. All plants look their best at a certain time of year. If any plant is of particular interest, check when it is in season, especially if you have to travel any distance to photograph it.

Original effects can be created by isolating one plant in a mass of others, perhaps using the shallow depth of field afforded by a telephoto lens. There are other opportunities for unusual viewpoints; for instance a plant or group of flowers, or even trees in the foreground of a scene adds interest in its own right and can also mask an unwanted object that would otherwise spoil the picture.

● BELOW By using extension rings it was possible to get very close to this marigold. Depth of field was very limited and a long exposure was needed. This meant that the camera had to be mounted on a tripod and a shield used to protect the plant from wind, so that it did not move and blur the picture.

CLOSE-UPS

- If you are taking close-ups of flowers, depth of field will be very small, especially if you are using extension rings or bellows. You will therefore need to stop down as much as possible, and to use a long exposure. If there is even the slightest breeze the plant will have to be sheltered from it, or it will sway and blur the picture.

- Lighting can also be a problem when working so close. If you are using available daylight you must take care not to cast a shadow from yourself or your equipment. A ring flash could be a useful accessory. This gives powerful but almost shadowless illumination. The flash tube forms a complete ring around the lens. Units for 35 mm cameras are quite compact and do not weigh very much.

- A tripod is essential because of the length of exposures.

- Details of trees and other plants are also excellent subjects for close-up shots. The texture of bark can be fascinating, and different shots can be mounted together to make a striking collage.

- ABOVE RIGHT Look for the unusual. There will always be something of interest on a country walk. This whitebell was growing alone in a sea of ordinary bluebells. Careful use of depth of field has put the background out of focus, making the flower even more prominent in the picture.

- RIGHT The texture of tree bark can be very satisfying, especially when several varieties are mounted together. A whole series of pictures can be built up over the years. This applies equally to many other natural forms.

- LEFT These cacti in the foreground frame the view. Not only do plants in the foreground add to the general composition, they can also be used to hide unsightly objects such as telegraph poles.

• BELOW Safari parks provide ample opportunity for photographing wildlife. A telephoto lens is essential as animals like this lion can only be photographed from a safe distance. Sometimes autofocus lenses do not work effectively when photographing through glass objects like car windows. Manual focusing can overcome this problem.

One of the most demanding areas of photography is that of wild or semi-wild animals. Patience is required, and a certain amount of forward planning is useful if not essential. Despite the arduous nature of this area, the rewards can certainly make it worthwhile. While most people do not have the opportunity to travel to the regions best suited to photography of big game or endangered species, many may live within reach of a farm or a safari or wildlife park. Safari parks have many exotic animals and with some peaceful species such as the zebra or giraffe it is sometimes possible to leave the vehicle and stand in the same area to take the shot with a medium telephoto lens of 100–200 mm.

• ABOVE If taking a photograph in a safari or wildlife park or zoo, a natural image is perfectly possible as long as the background includes relevant vegetation rather than an unsightly man-made intrusion. A close-up shot can be obtained without frightening the animal by using a 100 mm lens.

• ABOVE Small details are always most effective, especially when photographing fauna. These flamingoes look as if they are asleep yet a careful look at the far bird shows that its eye is open. This shot was taken with a 250 mm lens since if the camera had been positioned any closer the birds would have moved away.

PHOTOGRAPHING WILD ANIMALS

- Spend some time observing the behaviour of the animal; watch to see whether it is easily startled, or whether it appears to move in a constant direction.

- Try to select a viewpoint with an interesting background without unsightly fences or buildings.

- Be patient. Calling or gesturing to an animal will probably cause it to run in the opposite direction. Upsetting wild animals can also be dangerous: however docile they may seem it is important to remember that they are wild. It is best to avoid annoying both the animal and the farmer or ranger.

● BELOW Always be on the look out for spontaneous pictures. A quick check for any unsightly intrusions is usually all that is needed towards the composition of such shots.

● ABOVE This shot of cattle was taken in close from a higher viewpoint. All detail has been cropped out leaving only the black and white hides visible. This technique produces some effective graphic images that usually need a second look before the viewer realizes what the apparently abstract image is.

● RIGHT This shot was taken from a low viewpoint with a wide angle lens. This produces a dramatic image of the sky. By getting into position and being patient it is relatively easy to obtain effective and at times amusing shots of certain animals, whose natural curiosity means that they eventually come close to the camera for a better look. In this shot, the shutter was fired when the cow was about 3 ft (1 m) from the camera.

STILL LIFE

● BELOW By cropping the picture tightly – a medium telephoto lens was used – any extraneous details can be excluded. The texture of the wall provides a perfect canvas for setting off the doorway, the shrub and the traffic sign.

Travel often has the effect of making us more visually alert. Many things in our day-to-day lives may pass us by without us giving them a second glance. However, a new environment provides visual stimuli; to the photographer these stimuli provide a new awareness of photographic possibilities. Many items around us may not be very interesting in themselves, but gathered together in a collection, perhaps as a grouping of souvenirs from a particular place and photographed in an attractive way, a still life picture is created.

Still life arrangements have inspired painters throughout time and the same inspiration provides photographers with numerous creative opportunities. It is a useful discipline to look closely at, and arrange and light a group of inanimate objects. Sometimes these arrangements already exist and all that is required is to see the potential for an attractive shot.

● LEFT This is a good example of a ready-made still life. All the objects were fixed to the side of a barn on a ranch in Arizona. This shot frames them to their best advantage; no other preparation was needed. To the ranch owners this was just an assortment of objects rather than a creative arrangement. It is often worth looking around at familiar objects to view them with a fresh eye.

● RIGHT Some still life arrangements present themselves; this collection of African craft objects and furniture was lying in the corner of a room, lit by weak sunlight coming through an open window. A white reflector to the right helped throw back just enough light to illuminate the shadow areas.

● BELOW RIGHT A large aperture was used to emphasize the colour of these flowers by minimizing depth of field and throwing the background out of focus. The lines of the steps beyond are still just discernible and lift the background so that it remains a composite part of the picture without being too bland.

CHECKLIST FOR STILL LIFE SHOTS

● Should the arrangement be lit with flash or is there enough available light?

● Examine the available light for any creative elements: does a shaft of light fall at just the right angle?

● Which angle would look best for the shot? Imagine the arrangement in the centre of a circle. Stand a certain distance from the objects and walk around them slowly, stopping at regular intervals. Every pause provides a new visual angle and a different shot.

● Which viewpoint? Consider the arrangement from eye level, as well as from above and from below.

● Every visual angle provides a different background: which one is most suitable and complements the objects most effectively?

● Consider the depth of field: should the background be sharp or blurred?

PATTERNS

The refreshingly new viewpoints that travel often provides may reveal scenes or details that appear isolated from their immediate surroundings. This might be due to the way the light falls or may be because of an object's texture, or a combination of both these elements. Such images need not be confined to a documentary record of a place but can be used to startling creative effect. Examine the patterns created by an object or group of objects; often when such objects or scenes are carefully framed they form an interesting composition. Sometimes the pictures have a very abstract appearance or they may need careful viewing to see exactly what they are.

It is important to examine all the possibilities of a scene before taking the shot:

- Would it look best if framed symmetrically?

- Do the lines of perspective increase or decrease with the chosen viewpoint? If so, which is best?

- Is texture an important part of the picture? If so, does the light need to come from the back or the side to emphasize the texture?

- Would going in close help to achieve the effect better than being positioned further back?

- Would using a wide angle or a fisheye lens create a more interesting or subtle effect? This can be especially striking when looking up at the ceiling of a building, for instance, particularly if all the horizontal and vertical lines have been carefully aligned.

- Consider using prints or transparencies in a collage of different patterns. Try reversing one of the pictures and butting it up to one that is the correct way round.

120

All over the world events take place which are worth a special journey. One such is London's Notting Hill Carnival, the largest street festival in Europe. People flock from far afield to see the parade, dance and share the street parties. Some come for that reason alone, others as part of a wider tour of the city or the country.

GETTING IT RIGHT

If you decide to make an event the high point of your trip, a little planning will avoid disappointment. Make sure you arrive at the right time: this may sound obvious, but events do not always happen on the same date each year, especially if they are associated with a movable festival such as Easter (which also happens on a later date for the Orthodox Church).

Take plenty of film. This will help to keep your pictures consistent, as they will all be from the same emulsion batch. With film bought locally you can never be sure how long it has been lying around in the shop, perhaps exposed to damaging heat. You often see film being hawked around tourist sites unshielded from the blazing sun.

Professionals keep their film refrigerated. You cannot take a refrigerator with you, but at least you can keep your film as cool as possible.

CHOOSING A THEME

At huge and varied events it is difficult to get just one picture that says everything. That is not to say that you should not look out for such a shot. A better approach might be to shoot as much as you possibly can, and to assemble these pictures as a montage on a particular theme, or a diary of events. Themes could be faces, floats, costumes, food, or the onlookers themselves. Many events last for several days, so you will have plenty of time to get all your shots.

SECURITY

Events such as the Carnival are also a magnet for pickpockets. If you are carrying a case for accessories keep it properly secured at all times. Be alert for children who beg you to take their picture. It sometimes happens that, while you are concentrating on the shot, one of their colleagues is lifting your valuables.

● A collection of images placed together effectively captures the atmosphere of London's Notting Hill Carnival. Small details can be placed next to wider shots of dancers and street scenes to convey the sense of colour and exuberance.

SUPERMALT NO MALT DRINK

The Royal Borough of Kensington

POWIS GARDENS. W.11.

MAKING A PICTURE SERIES

When you are photographing an event you need to consider how many different things are happening. Sometimes there is so much diversity that you are spoilt for choice. In other instances the focus of interest may be narrow, and you will need to shoot from as many viewpoints as possible to give an informative account of the occasion.

PLANNING IN ADVANCE

It is always helpful to try to reconnoitre the place beforehand. Once the event begins you may not be able to move about easily, especially if you are burdened with a camera case and a tripod. In such a situation, try to pick a spot that will give you a good view of the main action. Also find out when the event is to begin, so that you can be there

• ABOVE As well as taking a formal picture of the troops standing to attention, for instance, try to move in close so that either the detail of the uniforms is visible or so that the impression of them marching close together is conveyed.

• ABOVE A crowd scene completes the picture. However, instead of merely photographing a mass of people, try to find a point of focus such as the young girl on her father's shoulders.

● LEFT At an event such as London's the Trooping the Colour, try to look for an unobtrusive background so that a group, such as these soldiers, stand out clearly. Sometimes extra height is needed for a particular shot: here the photographer stood on a strong camera case to gain an uninterrupted view over the heads of the people in front.

in plenty of time to get a good position at the front of the crowd. It is surprising how early people start to congregate for spectacles such as London's Trooping the Colour shown here.

If you cannot get a commanding view, try to take a small, lightweight set of steps. Not only will you be able to see over people's heads, you may also get an unusual angle on the proceedings.

Also try to work out beforehand which will be the key shots that you simply must have. You could make a list just in case, in the heat of the moment, you forget what you meant to do. This may seem obsessive, but hardly anyone makes a movie without a script. For example, at the Trooping the Colour you might plan to capture:

● the main participant – the Queen;
● a range of shots of the soldiers – individual guardsmen, and rows marching and standing to attention;
● the crowd itself.

This does not sound like a lot, but it is amazing how quickly an event can pass by and suddenly be over; it can seem like seconds if you have stood waiting for it for hours.

EQUIPMENT

Have a range of lenses, or if possible two camera bodies with zoom lenses – one could be 28–80 mm, the other 100–300 mm. In this way you will be able to work quickly with the minimum of weight. A monopod will help you to brace the camera. This is especially important if the weather is dull so that a long exposure is needed.

● LEFT An essential shot at an event like this is the main participant – in this case, the Queen. Try to plan ahead and think where the person will be: here she is taking the salute before retiring to Buckingham Palace.

● BELOW By using a more powerful telephoto lens it is possible to photograph the other participants, such as the members of the Royal Family.

Photographing People

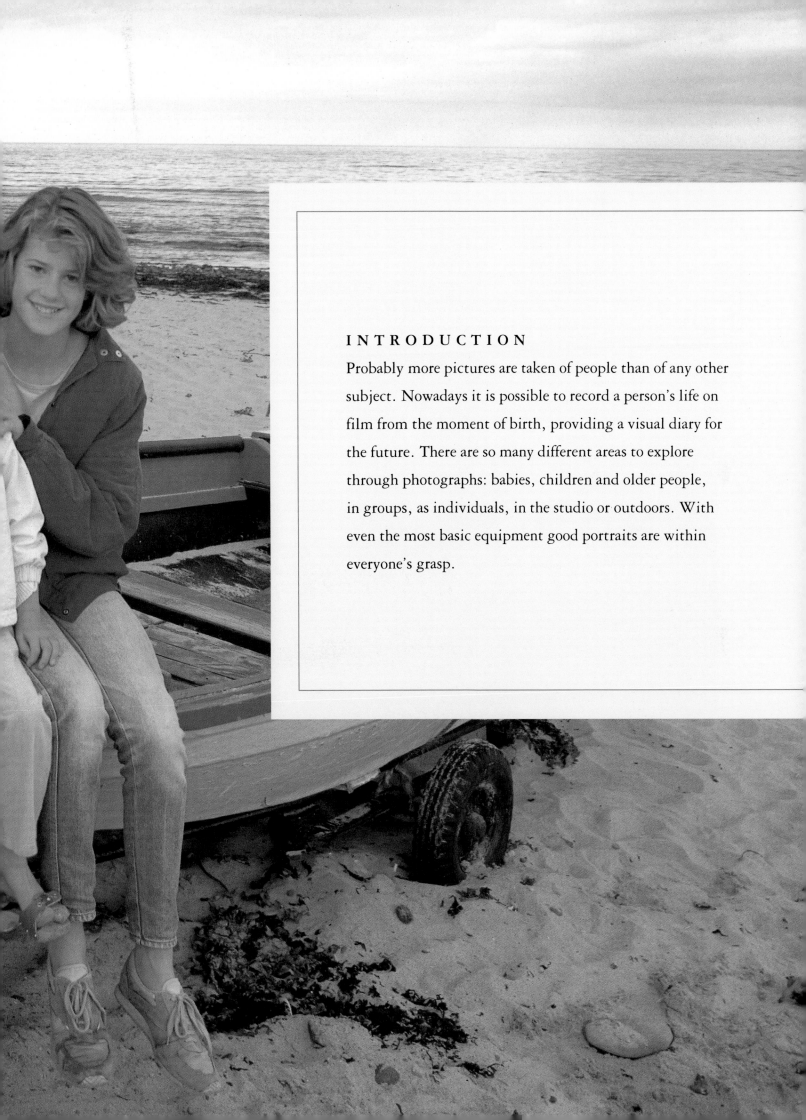

INTRODUCTION

Probably more pictures are taken of people than of any other subject. Nowadays it is possible to record a person's life on film from the moment of birth, providing a visual diary for the future. There are so many different areas to explore through photographs: babies, children and older people, in groups, as individuals, in the studio or outdoors. With even the most basic equipment good portraits are within everyone's grasp.

PORTRAITS: BACKGROUNDS

A key element in shooting a portrait is the care given to the background. Yet so often it is given very little thought and the finished photograph is spoilt by unwanted distractions. In some situations, such as in a studio, the background can be altered at will and could range from a simple plain white or black backdrop to a more elaborate purpose-built set, or even a back screen projection.

When photographing people in their homes, at the workplace or outdoors, it is important to use the existing environment to the best advantage. This may mean including the work the person does — or even a relevant hobby or collection — without letting the subject become a secondary element within the picture. Positioning plays a key role in creating a background: thought should be given to where the subject of the portrait is to sit or stand, as well as the distance and angle of the camera in relation to both the person and the background. Choice of aperture is another consideration to be taken into account; a small aperture will produce a greater depth of field than a large one, and so more of the background will be in focus which may well prove distracting.

● ABOVE Here the glass panels of the door make an interesting background without becoming an intrusion. They are slightly out of focus but they are still identifiable. This makes the child's face appear to spring out from the doorway as if one has captured her in a game of hide and seek.

● ABOVE The Russian poet Yevgeny Yevtushenko in his Moscow apartment. Although the background is very busy his collection of paintings is highlighted as well as him. By placing the poet in the centre of the frame with the relative neutrality of his dining table directly behind, he stands out and the eye is immediately drawn to him.

● RIGHT This picture of a model was achieved by placing her on a background of shiny plastic. The lighter blue stripes were placed diagonally on the darker stripes and the colours were chosen to complement her make up. This hardly elaborate but highly effective background shows what can be done to obtain an eyecatching shot without spending a great deal of money.

● LEFT This shot of a woman on a fairground stall in Tenerife illustrates an instance where the exception proves the rule. The background dominates the picture and the stallholder looks completely lost. However, because of the garishness of the display and its overwhelming dimensions the woman appears about to be buried in an avalanche of her own wares – adding a touch of humour to an otherwise rather mundane fairground scene.

PORTRAITS: PROPS

Props are items introduced into photographs that can either add something to the composition or tell us more about the person featured, perhaps providing information about a job or a hobby. Used successfully, props should enhance the picture without overpowering the person. In their simplest form props might be an addition to the clothes someone is wearing – a hat or a flower for instance. Sometimes a bunch of flowers placed in a vase near the subject will give a certain 'lift' to the shot. It could be that by placing people against a backdrop of their work the item they produce or create becomes a prop in itself.

In a working environment there are endless possibilities for adding available props to a shot. These may take the form of a background or may completely surround the subject. If the people featured are in an active position, do not pull back so far that they become insignificant. In situations like this it is possible that the prop can subtly convey the atmosphere rather than becoming a visually dominating part of the picture.

For instance, if a man is involved in working with molten metal, heated in a furnace, it would be the sensation of the intense heat rather than a prominent shot of the furnace that would say far more about the atmosphere. Going in close to the man and showing the heat reflected on his brow while keeping the furnace in the background, you could create an evocative composition.

As a photographer, always look for props in the immediate situation and employ them in the same way as an imported accessory.

● LEFT This shot was taken in a 'smoker', the room in which kippers are cured. The room had jet black walls and was quite small. By placing the owner in front of several rows of newly-smoked kippers the fish themselves provided the props to illustrate his work.

● LEFT Upon entering this tobacconist's shop it seemed that the entire place was full of props. Positioning the owner, lighting his pipe, among his wares added an extra visual dimension to the shot as well as conveying his character.

● ABOVE Costume can provide effective props in portraits; here the simple inclusion of an unusual hat changes the character of the shot and its subject.

● ABOVE This woman lived in a small apartment. She made exotic and expensive clothes and the purpose of the shot is to show her and her work together. Since her work is so colourful, it was decided to use it to fill the room and to cover the kitchen worktop in the foreground. The room takes on a swirl of colour but the woman remains a prominent part of the shot.

PORTRAITS: SELECTING A VIEWPOINT

Taking good shots of people depends on many factors. One of the most important is where you take the picture from. It is difficult to set down hard and fast rules about this, and obviously it depends on the situation. But one or two general points are always worth bearing in mind.

If you choose a high viewpoint to photograph a person full length this will have the effect of shortening them. But if you kneel down you will exaggerate their height. A quick look in any fashion magazine shows many examples of this stance, with models who appear to have legs that go on and on. With young children and babies it may be necessary to get down on the ground and choose an extremely low viewpoint for an effective shot.

When photographing groups or crowds of people it is generally best if you can remove yourself from the throng and view them from a distance, or perhaps from above.

At a special event you may be able to emphasize the detail of a uniform or costume to make an individual or small group stand out from the rest.

When you go in close the viewpoint you take can emphasize or exaggerate a person's expression. But remember that if you go too close with a wide angle lens it is very easy to get distortion, which may not look too flattering.

Your next consideration is exposure. If people are moving about rapidly TTL metering may be an asset, but when taking shots by this method beware: the meter is reading for the general scene and not for a predominantly dark or light area which may be the centre of interest of the picture. You may need to compensate for this to get a correct exposure.

● ABOVE At formal events like the Trooping the Colour in London it sometimes pays to look for a different angle as well as the more obvious shots. A viewpoint behind this guardsman emphasizes the colour and detail of his uniform. The line of soldiers can be seen out of focus in the background, which helps to concentrate attention on him.

● LEFT Going low and looking up at this man's face has helped to highlight his features and expression. He is playing chess and I wanted to capture his concentration. If people are wearing hats be careful that the brim does not cast an unwanted shadow across their face.

● LEFT This shot was taken from ground level, lying in a similar position to that of the boy. The emphasis is on his face and this has been exaggerated by going in close. Using an 85 mm lens at this distance has helped to reduce distortion and has put the background slightly out of focus so that nothing distracts us from his gaze.

● BELOW It is very difficult to get a general shot of people from ground level in a crowded place, such as a bustling market scene. This shot shows as many people as possible, with the stalls and some of the goods they sold and was taken from a communal balcony. From here a downwards viewpoint was obtained of the shoppers milling back and forth. The angle the shot was taken from makes a strong diagonal of the crowd that enhances the overall composition.

MAKE-UP

Taking spontaneous pictures of friends and relatives produces natural and pleasing results. The appeal may come from seeing them in an unexpected situation, pulling a face, or seeing something that makes their hair stand on end. But often when taking a special portrait a little extra is required. A girlfriend, wife or daughter may be seen as an attractive person, but will the camera see her in the same way?

Often what is needed is suitable make-up. The subject may already wear make-up, but often this is inappropriate for photographic purposes. Professional photographers taking fashion and beauty pictures work with make-up artists and hair stylists. These highly trained people have spent years perfecting their craft and they can literally transform a model to give any required look.

Obviously this is the top end of the market, and no amateur would be expected to know or hire such experts. But it is worthwhile studying fashion magazines to get an idea of current looks, so that these can be discussed with the subject so that there is a good chance of getting the required effect.

Pay attention to detail. Even with the simplest make-up the shot can be ruined by a stray hair or crooked parting. Also make-up can be too reflective and cause unattractive highlights.

Men also need to take care with grooming. Messy hair and grubby fingernails are hardly the way to enhance a portrait, especially when going in close.

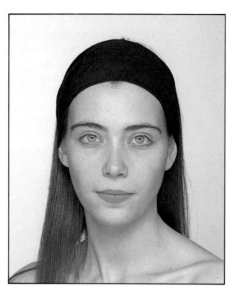

● At this stage the model is not wearing any make-up. She has used a cleanser to clean her face thoroughly, and is now ready to be made up.

● A little foundation has been applied. This gives the skin an all-over even tone. Translucent foundation cream has been used, matching the model's own natural skin colouring. Skin concealer cream can be used to cover any blemishes or shadows under the eyes. Powder is then applied to seal the foundation and to give the face a matt finish.

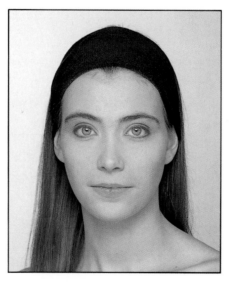

● The next stage is eye make-up. Here a little eye shadow and mascara have been used. Depending on the look required, false eyelashes could be added.

● Here the eyes have been finished with more mascara, and blusher has been applied. The lips have been outlined and covered in a pale base.

● The lips have been finished with lipstick. The model's hair has been brushed and she is now ready to be photographed.

Many people are daunted by the idea of taking photographs in the studio. But generally speaking, the majority find that handling studio lights is an easy skill to pick up.

Look through various magazines which feature pictures taken in a studio. The lighting techniques are as varied as the subjects they light. In some only one light is used, in others five or more.

The least expensive light available is a photoflood with a reflector and stand. But many people find the glare and heat from such lights uncomfortable. An alternative is studio flash. The units work from the mains and are much more powerful than a camera's built-in flash unit or one that fits onto a camera hot shoe. Each unit has its own power supply; some of the most powerful have attachments for additional flash heads.

As well as the standard reflector there is a whole variety of different attachments that can alter the character of the light. These include large umbrella-type reflectors in white, silver or gold, which bounce diffused light onto the subject, giving a softer light than a standard reflector.

An even softer light can be obtained by using a 'softbox'. These come in various sizes, but all work on the same principle. The box fits over the flash head. It has a highly reflective silver lining, and a diffusing material stretched over the front. Other diffusers can be stretched over the first one to diffuse the light even further.

Another lighting attachment is called a 'snoot'. This directs a thin beam of light onto the subject. It is not the same as a conventional spotlight, which has a broader beam which can be focused. Spotlights can also have inserts placed between the lamp and the lens, which throw patterns onto the lit area.

As with all accessories, special lights have to be used carefully and creatively. Used by themselves they will not produce miracles.

● LEFT Here only the background is lit, to make it white and silhouette the subject. This technique has to be used with care, because an overlit background can cause flare. When framing the subject take care that the light sources themselves do not creep into the picture.

● RIGHT Using just one light has lit one side of the model's face. This has left the other side of her face with dark, unattractive shadows, especially by the nose and eyes.

● LEFT A 'fill-in' light has been introduced on the left side. This is less powerful than the main light. It has softened the shadows without making the face look flat. A reflector would have a similar effect.

● RIGHT Another light has been used over the model's head to give more body to the hair. It was attached to a stand with a boom, an arm extending sideways. A boom allows a light to be brought close to a model without the stand appearing in the picture.

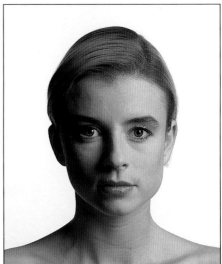

● The final picture has the addition of a white reflector placed under the model's face. This slightly softens the shadow under her chin, and to a lesser extent under her eyes.

PORTRAITS IN THE STUDIO

There are many advantages to taking portraits in a studio. For a start, the photographer has total control of the lighting, and the choice of backgrounds and props. Also, depending on the type of photograph, make-up and dress can be specified or chosen and altered.

Some photographers, and even more so their models, can feel inhibited by the studio environment, however. A bare room with only a few lights and rolls of background paper can seem an impossible setting for the creation of an interesting picture. But it only takes a little know-how and a measure of confidence to achieve a whole new dimension in photography.

Studios do not have to be elaborate, lofty or spacious. In fact, a reasonable-sized room in an ordinary house can work just as well as a studio, as the shot of the girl against a white background demonstrates.

To improvise a studio at home, hire lights from a professional photographic dealer, or perhaps buy one or two modest units as a start. However, good flash equipment would be a better investment than floodlights. It is generally more powerful, which allows shorter exposures than are possible with photofloods. It is also more comfortable to work with. Photofloods get very hot, and after a while this can make conditions uncomfortable. People also find the constant glare irritating.

An alternative is to hire a purpose-built studio. There are quite a number of these and they are advertised in photographic magazines. It is often a good idea to join a local photographic society, which can probably provide access to such facilities as well as equipment, assistance and even models.

● BELOW One of the advantages of taking pictures in a studio is that seamless backgrounds can be made with long rolls of paper. These can be hung from the wall or ceiling, and extended along the ground to conceal visible corners. A hired studio should normally provide such backgrounds, though all the paper that is used has to be paid for.

● LEFT This man's face is lit with a very low-key light. This has heightened his features and given him an enigmatic expression. Working in a studio gives total control of light, and allows the mood of a picture to be altered. Another light with a snoot (this gives a directional beam) was projected onto the background to give a graduated appearance.

● BELOW This picture shows what can be done in the home. A length of white cotton material was pinned to the wall and draped over a sofa. One flash was used, fitted with a large diffuser called a softbox. This was powerful enough to illuminate both the girl and the background. Some people – both photographers and models – find it less intimidating to work in an ordinary home than in a proper photographic studio. But as confidence and adventurousness increase, an improvised home studio can become a restriction, unless of course the room is very large.

FORMAL PORTRAITS

Formal portraits do not mean that subjects have to sit or stand to attention so that they look stiff and uncomfortable. In the early days of photography when exposure times were measured in minutes people did have to sit very still to avoid blurring the picture. Photographers even used special clamps at the back of their sitter's neck and waist to brace them in position. Fortunately these days are long past.

The most important thing in any portrait, formal or otherwise, is to capture the expression that best illustrates a person's character or status, or both. However formal the portrait might be, try to enter into a dialogue with the sitter. Discover a common interest, and the conversation will become easy and relaxed.

Even if the sitter is a complete stranger, try to plan the general nature of the shot in advance. It makes a bad impression if the first thing the photographer does after meeting the sitter is to stare hard at him, as if undecided what to do. But it is also important to plan wisely; it produces an even worse impression if, after a few shots, it becomes clear that the setting does not work, so that all the equipment has to be altered.

Often, time is of the essence. Some people, such as businessmen and public figures, are very busy, and they may be under the impression that photographs can be taken as quickly as if they had walked into an automatic photo booth. Knowing what is wanted, and directing sitters with flair and firmness, can yield strong portraits in a relatively short time. The results will please them and enhance the photographer's reputation and they are more likely to return.

● ABOVE Although this portrait of a young girl was taken in a studio, it is full of flair and vitality. An immediate rapport was struck up with her so that she felt confident and relaxed. Atmosphere is very important in any situation where there is close communication between photographer and model. It would be disastrous to start a session in an atmosphere of tension; this is as true in the studio as it is on location.

● LEFT This room looks grand and formal, yet the woman's expression gives the portrait warmth and there is the impression that it was a relaxed photographic session. Both the room and the hallway which is visible through the far doorway had to be lit. If the door had been shut the atmosphere might have seemed a little claustrophobic. Being able to see beyond the room adds space and light. Although the picture takes a wide view, there is no doubt that the woman is the centre of attention.

● RIGHT Formality need not mean rigidity. In this portrait of the photographer Terence Donovan the composition's formality and symmetry give him an enigmatic quality. For those who do not know his reputation as a photographer there are a few props to give a clue to his profession. Terence Donovan also runs a very successful film production company, and there is just a hint of the entrepreneur here.

● RIGHT The portrait of the former Speaker of the House of Commons in London had to be taken in a 10-minute session. His gown and wig might have made him look intimidating and rigid; instead they signify the status of his position and are in keeping with a portrait that is both formal and interesting. Although the Speaker appears small this is in effective contrast to the grandeur of the room.

INFORMAL PORTRAITS

Many portraits work because they have an informal look that most people would call 'natural'. But even pictures like these need thought to make them successful. For instance, it is pointless to take lots of pictures in a casual manner if the exposure or focus are incorrect or the shot is badly composed. With a little forethought all these problems can be avoided, but at the same time there is no need to be so preoccupied with the mechanics of photography that it causes inhibition and the pictures become rigid and unspontaneous.

As with all aspects of photography, the most important thing is being so familiar with the equipment that all the controls become second nature. Once these are mastered it is possible to concentrate on technique and become more adventurous.

This might mean experimenting with a different type of film. Try a high-speed one such as 1600 ISO. This will give very grainy results, but that is by no means an unattractive effect, as one of the pictures here shows. Also, using such a fast film allows pictures to be taken in almost any conditions. The film can even be uprated to 3200 ISO. (Remember that if this is done the whole film has to be shot at this rating, and when giving the film to the processing laboratory the technicians must be told that it has been uprated so that they can increase development time.)

A zoom lens, especially when combined with an autofocus mechanism, makes for faster work since focal length can be changed without the need to swap lenses.

Ultimately, of course, it is the photographer's eye that seizes upon that good shot, however much advanced equipment may be available!

● ABOVE This picture radiates spontaneity, warmth and humour. It is a good example of capturing the moment, which swiftly passes when dealing with animals. Going in close helps the general composition and focuses attention on the woman and the chicken.

● BELOW Pictures like these come readily to the alert photographer. Always have the camera loaded with film to avoid wasting time. The person might move away – or in this case merely put on his socks and shoes.

● ABOVE An ultra-fast film, 1600 ISO, has perfectly caught this young boy's cheeky expression. The grainy quality of the film, far from being a drawback, adds to the picture. The day was dull and the area surrounded by trees, so it is unlikely that a slow film would have given an adequate picture. Especially with informal portraits, be ready to try something different and do not be afraid to push film to its limits.

● RIGHT This couple was photographed informally at a barbecue. Using a 100 mm lens makes them fill the frame without the need to go so close as to make them feel uncomfortable. Her vivacious smile contrasts attractively with his rather whimsical expression. The result is a natural look that is relaxed and charming.

● BELOW Even when going in close, it is still possible to achieve a relaxed portrait. The old man's weathered face is set against a plain background which isolates and emphasizes his face. The ladder acts as a prop and introduces an informal element into the composition. The man's open-necked shirt adds a carefree element without looking untidy.

FULL-LENGTH PORTRAITS

Not all portraits of people need to be head and shoulders or full face. Sometimes the only way of achieving a good portrait is to photograph a person full length, and to include some of their environment.

When choosing a viewpoint for full-length portraits it is important to remember that photographing a standing person from low down will accentuate their height and make their legs look longer. Conversely, photographing the same person from a high viewpoint, looking down on them, will foreshorten them and make their legs look shorter.

When using a wide angle lens, care must be taken if the person is placed at the side of the frame. Some wide angle lenses, especially very wide angle ones, distort the extreme edges so that, for instance, a face will look 'stretched'.

When photographing a group of people full length, make sure that all

● LEFT This spontaneous full-length portrait was taken on a drive through Greece. The low viewpoint makes the bale of hay look even larger. The vibrant colour of the hay also makes an interesting background for the boy.

● BELOW In bright sunlight, be careful that ugly shadows do not fall across the faces of the subjects. In this picture the man was positioned in the doorway to keep the light evenly spread. Just moving someone back or forward could make all the difference. Do not be afraid to take control of the shot and direct people to the position where they will be seen to the best advantage.

● LEFT This picture of distillery workers was lit by flash. The warehouse was large, so they were grouped tightly in a confined space to give more or less even lighting. Also, they are placed quite close to the background so that the light does not fall off sharply behind them. In such situations, look carefully and try to get the best out of the environment.

● BELOW This full-length portrait was taken from a high viewpoint. By sitting the woman in a chair the problem of foreshortening has been avoided. The camera was on a tripod in a fixed position, so that items could be moved around the room till they looked right in the viewfinder. Even the dog let itself be placed so that it looks as if it was posing for the camera.

their faces can be seen. This is not just a case of careful positioning, but also of making sure that the shadow cast by one person does not fall across the face of another.

If the portrait is lit by flash make sure that this is spread evenly. Many built-in flash systems do not produce a very powerful light. A person standing in a large room may be well lit but the background will be dark and murky, because the flash was not powerful enough to light the whole room.

When photographing people full length outdoors in bright sunshine, be careful if anyone is wearing a hat. The brim can cast a dark shadow on the face. If necessary use fill-in flash to soften this shadow and eliminate the possibility of obscuring the facial expression.

PEOPLE IN THE HOME

● BELOW Children like helping around the house and such occasions can provide good opportunities for pictures, especially if there is a camera loaded and ready. Even better, this should be a simple model that anyone can use. If it is loaded with medium to fast film such as 200 ISO, it should cope with most situations without flash being necessary.

Many people do not take pictures at home except on special occasions such as a birthday or Christmas. But there are many other times when opportunities for photographs present themselves, and often these can lead to excellent portraits. One advantage of taking pictures at home is that people feel relaxed because they are in their normal environment. Another is that they are surrounded by objects that reflect their personality, which can be brought into pictures as props or backgrounds; these will reveal the varied aspects of their way of life, and their interests.

There is plenty of opportunity for spontaneous pictures in the home, especially of children. They may be doing the most ordinary, everyday things but even these, when viewed through the camera, can be seen in a new light, and spontaneous actions captured. This is one reason why it is so important to be ready with your camera. If it seems laborious to get out all your equipment, one solution is to buy an inexpensive compact camera for use around the house. This can always be kept loaded and ready to hand. It should have a built-in flash for quick shots in all conditions. In this way there will never be a reason to miss a picture – and many pictures will be well worth the effort.

● BELOW This informal picture of a young girl at the piano needed flash. The piano keys make an interesting background. The high viewpoint adds to the picture's informality.

● BELOW LEFT This couple photographed in their conservatory is a good example of balancing flash with daylight. The picture looks as if everything is lit by daylight, but in fact if flash had not been added the foreground and the couple's faces would have been in deep shadow. It was a day of patchy cloud with the sun going in and out, so it needed patience to wait for the sun to shine – but the result was worth it.

● BELOW Although this portrait is posed it has a relaxed feel to it. The musical scores in the foreground hint that the subject is a composer, or at least that music is important to him. Two flash units were used. One was directed at the man and the foreground, the other to light the area behind. These were balanced so that the scene outside the window was correctly exposed as well.

OUTDOOR PORTRAITS

● BELOW Even on a dull overcast day good pictures can be taken. Photographing this person out walking her dog against a wooded background has cut out the dull sky. A 250 mm lens has reduced the depth of field, so that the focus is firmly on the subject.

Bright, sunny days offer good opportunities for taking portraits outdoors. But they can cause problems too. Bright sunlight can create harsh shadows. It can also make people screw up their eyes and squint, which looks most unattractive. To get round this problem, try to move the person being photographed into an area of shade. Alternatively, turn them away from direct sunlight and use a reflector to throw light back into their face. If the person is wearing a hat and the brim is casting a shadow across their face, use fill-in flash to soften the shadow.

Another problem with portraits outdoors is that the wind blows people's hair about and leaves it looking messy. If possible, look for an area sheltered from the wind.

Be on the look-out for appealing backgrounds. This could be something with an interesting texture, such as a stone wall, or it might be a view into a landscape. If the background is not photogenic, consider ways of cutting it out. This can be done by going in close and framing the picture tightly, or by using a large aperture to throw the background out of focus.

When photographing groups of people make sure that one does not cast an ugly shadow on another.

Bright but hazy days give an even, shadowless light, but in certain conditions and with some colour films the results may be a little cool. To alleviate this problem try using an 81A filter. This will slightly warm up the tones.

● RIGHT These young girls form a well-proportioned group. They were photographed with the sun to one side and slightly behind them. This has avoided ugly shadows under their eyes, and stopped any one of them from shading another. The background is dominated by the pool; the wall is unobtrusive and does not spoil the composition.

● LEFT Focusing directly on this man's eyes shows the full character of his face. Every detail of his beard is sharp. He was photographed under a white blind that acted as a diffuser so that the light, although bright, does not cast any shadows on his face.

● ABOVE In this picture of an elderly woman, a 100 mm medium telephoto lens combined with a wide aperture has put the background out of focus. It has made the splash of green behind the subject unobtrusive, but the colour complements that of her headscarf. She is in a relatively shaded area, so that her face glows with an even, natural light.

● RIGHT A low viewpoint and going in quite close lets this boy dominate the picture. The surrounding landscape gives a feeling of spring, and the boy's expression is one of playfulness. When taking portraits out of doors experiment with different viewpoints. Otherwise pictures will have an air of sameness.

PEOPLE IN THEIR ENVIRONMENT

Photographing people in their own environment can be very rewarding, especially when you are on holiday. Generally strangers are only too willing to be in your shots – particularly if they are in an area where tourists are commonplace. However, if you want to photograph someone close in you should always ask their permission first. There are several reasons for this:

- It is polite. If your manner is friendly they will not feel threatened.

- Once they know they are the centre of interest in your photograph, they are much more likely to do what you ask of them. This is important because, although they may be attractive and their environment interesting, they may be standing in a less than ideal place and would be much better framed if you asked them to move slightly to one side, or perhaps onto a step. You might be able to get a better background by moving yourself, but if you creep about in a furtive manner you are likely to upset them and make them uncooperative if you do finally decide to ask them to move. In this case you will have lost the chance of a good photograph.

- Once you have gained their confidence, they may show you another area or aspect of their lives which you would otherwise overlook. This may well prove more interesting than the original scene.

- Having gained their cooperation and moved them into the position you want, look carefully at the light falling on their faces. Are they in bright sun which creates ugly shadows under their eyes and noses? Or is the sun behind them and shining into the lens? In either case do not be afraid to move them again. You may never get another chance.

● BELOW This woman was cracking almonds outside her house. Her position was fine, but she was in strong shadow. By placing a small portable reflector to the right of the camera, just enough light was bounced back onto her. This is an example of a situation where a very bright background can give a misleading exposure reading.

● BELOW This shot is a good example of the advantages of taking people into your confidence. This shop was a good photographic setting but inside, where this couple was, it was too dark. The couple agreed to move into the doorway where the light was better than within the shop, but the shot still needed something more, so they also agreed to hang sausages around the doorway. As a final touch, they are holding one of their whole hams. A bit of friendly discussion produced a shot which would not have existed otherwise.

● ABOVE Markets, like this souk in Agadir, Morocco, provide a wealth of opportunities for the alert photographer. This young boy was leading his camel through the throng of people gathered around the vendors. He is dwarfed by his camel, which has a typically arrogant expression. In situations like this feel free to move around the person until he is in the best position with the light. The other people in the souk fill the background, but are out of focus so they do not intrude.

● LEFT Although the picture was taken from some distance, these security guards at the Museum of Art in Washington DC were well aware that they were being photographed, and they played to the camera. Their presence emphasized the monumentality of the bronze sculpture that serves as a backdrop. Always be on the look-out for such a juxtaposition.

PHOTOGRAPHING PEOPLE

Poor weather does not have to deter you from photographing people. Sometimes it can actually add to and animate a photograph. But before taking your camera out in pouring rain, remember that cameras should not get wet. A camera that gets thoroughly soaked – or worse still, dropped in the sea – will probably be irreparably damaged.

If the skies are full of fast-moving clouds with quick bursts of intermittent sunshine, extra care will have to be taken with exposure. If the sun is out when you take your reading but behind cloud when you take your shot, the photograph will be underexposed. The reverse will be true if the sun is obscured when you take your reading but then comes out before you take your shot.

Look out for something unusual that will lift your shots in poor weather, and give them a point of interest. An isolated colour, or a solitary figure in a landscape, will dispel the grey look. Whatever happens, do not be deterred by poor weather conditions.

● LEFT Here is a good example of making the best of a picture in poor weather, as people cross Dublin's Halfpenny Bridge in the pouring rain, their umbrellas jostling for space. The two large coloured umbrellas stand out in an otherwise monochromatic scene. The picture was taken inside a doorway which helped protect the camera from the rain.

● ABOVE As you go for a walk on a dull, overcast day, you are all the more likely to notice a splash of colour that can make all the difference to a photograph. The flag on the beach marked the area of safe bathing. It was pure coincidence that the red and yellow of the flag matched the colours of the children's oilskins. Even something as simple as a patch of colour can enliven the dullest of scenes. Be prepared at all times for the chance of a spontaneous shot.

KEEPING YOUR CAMERA DRY

- If you are with other people, have them hold an umbrella over you. If not, try to stand beneath some shelter.

- A lens hood will protect your lens from rain. If the lens does get splashed, wipe the drops off immediately with a soft cloth or lens tissue. If you do not do this, they will show up on your photographs as unsightly out-of-focus blobs.

- A plastic bag put over the camera when you are not using it provides quite good protection from the wet.

● ABOVE A close-up of a girl in the pouring rain shows just how animated a poor-weather shot can be. Her brilliant smile and bright eyes express fun and cheerfulness, even though she is getting soaked. Going in close puts the emphasis on her rather than the dreary background. A lens hood protected the lens from splashes.

● RIGHT Although this shot was taken in the summer a dull sea mist was drifting inland from the coast. The isolation of the child looking for shells on the beach is emphasized by the mist. The Victorian railway viaduct in the background helps to relieve the gloom. If there had been more people in this shot they would have distracted from the image of the private world the child inhabits.

HOLIDAYS

More photographs are taken on holiday than at any other time. Obviously there is an incentive to get good shots of family or friends, not to mention new and interesting buildings and scenes.

There are a few points to remember before setting off: take plenty of film; make sure that all equipment is in working order and that any batteries are fresh. For a beach holiday, take a plastic bag to protect the camera from sand as it can ruin lenses. If any gets on the front element, blow it off – cleaning the lens with a cloth would have the same effect as sandpapering it.

Bright sunlight can cast deep and unattractive shadows under people's eyes so it is important to think about portable lighting equipment. Flash can be used to fill in these shadows. Another solution is to use a reflector to throw light back onto the subject's face. At the seaside there are vast areas that reflect light, and it is easy to be misled by the reading given by a light meter. If possible take a meter reading from a neutral area.

Look out for spontaneous shots. Candid shots, even of total strangers, can make a good picture – competitions have been won by such pictures so be prepared for that instant shot.

Wherever the scene of the holiday, it is likely that there will be some event such as a fair or festival. These provide local colour, and should be used to advantage. They can include information about customs and traditions which adds an air of authenticity and situation to the shot.

● LEFT Young children make delightful subjects, none more so than this boy with his bucket. Be careful with exposure in seaside shots, since the glare from the sea and beach can fool the meter into underexposing the subject.

● RIGHT These children were on a Romany caravan holiday in Ireland. They were slightly reluctant to be photographed, but agreed as long as the horse and caravan were included in the shot.

● BELOW Although slightly posed, this picture of a young girl at a swimming pool is an attractive holiday portrait. The line of the white wall adds to the composition and makes an effective contrast with the blue of the pool. Shots like this can be fun, but it is important to work quickly so that being photographed does not become a chore for the child – boredom cannot be disguised.

● BELOW In the holiday season most countries provide good set-piece events. Events can happen spontaneously, so be prepared. It is important to get the best viewpoint for a shot, as far as this can be done without being rude or pushy. Failing this, hold the camera above the heads of the crowd and point it at the action – it may be an outside chance, but it could work!

● ABOVE This picture taken from a high viewpoint shows what can be achieved by looking for a new and striking angle. Seen from above, the water is translucent. The dinghy adds a splash of colour. The two boys did not know they were being photographed, and the spontaneity of this simple shot adds to its effect.

● RIGHT This couple fits in well with most people's idea of the British on holiday. The photographer did not know the people, but they happily agreed to be photographed. The picture is full of good-natured humour. Only a camera ready for instant use will capture the mood in this way.

MOTHER AND CHILD

When photographing children it is often a good idea to include their mother. She is usually the closest person to the child and the best suited to allay its fears and put it at ease, and help it to adopt the best position.

Use a photographer's eye to look for the best viewpoint and lighting to show the natural bond between mother and child. As in any situation when photographing more than one person, be careful that the mother's head does not cast a shadow on the child's face.

If working indoors try to use available light. This will be less distracting to the child, which may be alarmed if flash is used. If flash is necessary, soften the light as much as possible. This can be done by bouncing the light off a suitable surface such as a white ceiling or board. Alternatively put a diffuser over the light. This can be tracing paper or even a handkerchief. Take care here not to underexpose the photograph. The best way to avoid this is to use a flash meter, which shows exactly how much light is falling on the subject. If the mother and child are sitting by a window, a reflector can be used to throw some natural light back on them.

When working out of doors make sure that neither the mother or child gets cold. Not only is it uncomfortable for them, but they might be shown with red hands and dripping noses.

Above all, be aware that most children can only concentrate for a short time. This may mean working quickly. Conversely, a good deal of patience may be required to catch the child at the best moment.

● ABOVE This was taken in a studio. Care was needed to keep the light from casting the mother's shadow onto the child. Placing the child behind the mother has created an informal mood and it looks as if a game is in progress. Try to make pictures look fun, especially in the artificial conditions of the studio.

● LEFT This picture was taken against the light and a reflector was used to bounce light back onto the mother and child. This has given a soft halo effect to their hair and made the picture look warm and summery. Asking them to lie down on the grass has further increased the air of a natural bond between mother and child. The low viewpoint makes the viewer feel part of the picture.

● RIGHT Draping a white sheet over the window has created a very soft background. The mother and child were lit by flash softened by a diffuser. This has softened the overall effect even more, perfectly fitting the mood. In this case the baby was fascinated by the flash light, and it proved a useful diversion for him. Using a 100 mm lens allowed a comfortable distance between the camera and the subject.

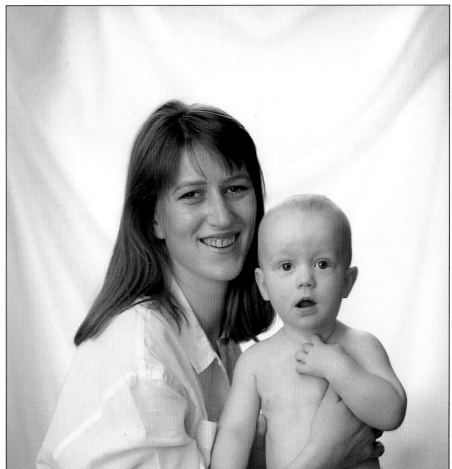

● LEFT Going in very close has achieved an intimate picture of a mother and her son. It was taken on a chilly autumn day, and they are huddled together to give a snug effect. In such situations take care that the child does not get too cold and become distressed.

BABIES AND YOUNG CHILDREN

Photographs of young children can bring pleasure to many people, not only their parents and close relatives.

The important thing to remember is that young children tire easily. Patience will be needed to get the best out of what might be a very brief photographic session. If the child seems to be becoming unhappy it is best to take a break and restart at a later time. Try to avoid dressing young children up in strange costumes, as these can humiliate them. The child should be having fun, and not be made fun of.

Natural light is probably the best, as it will not distract or distress the child. Very young babies are often upset by flashlight.

Try to think ahead about backgrounds. An ugly intrusion can ruin what would otherwise be a great shot, and there may not be a chance to move the subject. As well as more formal portraits, try to photograph the young child engaged in some activity – playing, or perhaps at bathtime.

When photographing small children in a studio or away from home, have a few toys around for them to play with. They may well not be able to understand a request to go to a particular place or do something specific. Often the only way of getting the right expression from a child is to play the fool.

With children who are two years old or more, Polaroid pictures can be a great help at the photography session. They will be fascinated by seeing the results instantly, and the pictures are also useful for checking exposure, lighting and general composition.

● BELOW Bathing can be fun for young children and provide plenty of opportunity for natural-looking pictures. This one was taken by standing directly over the bath and using the light coming in through a window. A standard focal length lens was used. By working quickly several good shots were taken with the minimum of fuss.

● ABOVE This child acted spontaneously for the camera in a studio which other children would have found daunting. Several shots were taken, each one with a different expression. They were lit by a flash unit which had a fast recycling time so that shots could be taken in close succession. Editing the pictures was difficult as each one had its own character, but this one was finally declared the winner.

● RIGHT Going in close on this baby's face has given full emphasis to his expression. Soft lighting has given a feeling of gentleness. A good deal of gesticulation, face pulling and cooing by the photographer and the child's parents were needed to maintain his interest. Never prolong a session with a young child to the point where it becomes upset. At the first sign of unhappiness, it is best to stop and try again later.

● LEFT The blanket makes an unusual and interesting background. Always look out for something new, so that shots taken over a period have variety. This picture was taken by natural light coming through a large window, with a reflector used to throw light back and give a fairly even level of illumination.

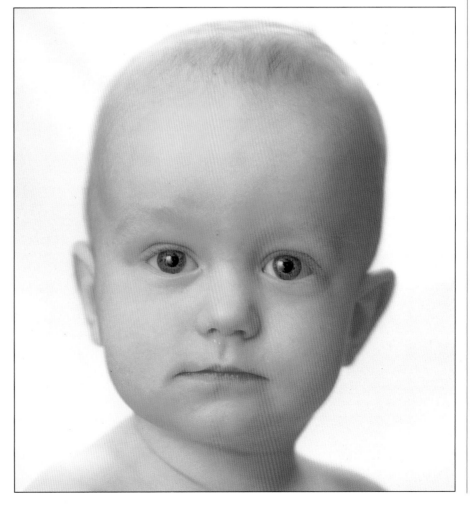

CHILDREN

Children are ideal subjects for photographs, for many reasons. First, such pictures tell the story of their lives. From the moment they are born there is a visual record of their development which will not only be a pleasure to their parents and grandparents but will also be fun for them to look back on, and to show their own children in years to come. Even with the arrival of home video cameras, it is hard to beat a still picture that captures a fleeting moment in a child's life. And last but not least, an unlimited number of copies can easily be made and sent to friends or relatives anywhere in the world.

There is no need to photograph every breath children take, but at least try to make a record of important events such as birthday parties. These in themselves will make a fascinating series of pictures that show the child growing and changing. It will also provide the children with pictures of their friends.

Often the best way to photograph children is to take a candid approach, especially when they are absorbed in some activity. A medium telephoto or zoom lens – 80 to 200 mm – will be useful in such cases, making it possible to keep at a certain distance but still fill the frame. A film with a speed of about 200 ISO should allow work in moderate lighting conditions without a tripod or flash, either of which could distract the child and destroy the spontaneity.

● RIGHT Special occasions such as birthday parties provide excellent opportunities for the photographer. This picture was lit entirely by the candles on the birthday cake. A 400 ISO film allowed an exposure just short enough for the camera to be hand-held. If flash had been used the atmosphere would have been killed, and the candles would have faded into insignificance. The picture also captures the birthday cake, over which a good deal of trouble has been taken.

● BELOW This portrait of a small girl captures a spontaneous expression that is at once both intimate and charming. The warm light and her yellow jumper make a pleasing contrast with her dark colouring. Always be on the look-out for quick shots like this.

● ABOVE Children's hobbies and pastimes provide many opportunities for pictures. Although this picture was taken in close the girl was not inhibited as she was happy to be photographed with her pony.

● RIGHT Children can become totally absorbed in what they are doing, shown in this picture of a young girl feeding pigeons. Standing back so as not to inhibit the subject usually makes for a better picture. A telephoto lens is useful in such situations, as it allows a frame-filling shot, perhaps without the child even being aware of the photographer. Patience is also needed, and can be richly rewarded.

CHILDREN AT PLAY

Children play naturally, so play gives good opportunities for natural pictures. Even in a favourite game children may lose interest in a few minutes, so quick work is needed to capture a good expression or gesture.

When working indoors, in the interests of speed it is probably best to use flash. This may upset a few children, but if they are busy they will probably take it in their stride. They may even be fascinated by it.

An alternative is to use a fast film and available light. If this is from an ordinary tungsten light bulb it will be necessary to balance daylight film with an 80A filter; otherwise the photograph will come out with an excessively warm, orange cast. There are now a few fast tungsten-balanced colour negative films, and a better selection of colour reversal ones. However, with these, if any other shots on the film are taken out of doors it will be necessary to use an 85B colour balancing filter to avoid a blue cast.

Try to think of different angles when photographing children at play. Consider a high viewpoint, looking down on them. This will make them look diminutive, but that may be an attractive effect. If the background is unsuitable, go in close to eliminate it, or use a large aperture so that it is out of focus. If the child is absorbed in painting or reading, try to get a shot that shows that concentration.

If the child gets bored, give up at once. Persistence will only produce tears of frustration and may put the child off further photographic sessions. A few Polaroid pictures taken to begin with will usually interest children and make them more patient when shots are taken with normal film.

● RIGHT, CENTRE AND BOTTOM LEFT These pictures were taken in a nursery school. The children liked being photographed; it was a new experience for them. However, young subjects can easily become bored and lose interest. Patience on the photographer's part is paramount in such situations.

● BELOW Although the ball is slightly blurred, this adds to the feeling of movement. The shot was taken at $1/125$ second. A faster speed might have frozen the ball and the feeling of action would have been lost.

● BELOW Sometimes the simplest shots are the most effective. This one of a young girl sitting on her bed surrounded by soft toys was taken using natural light streaming in from a window, diffused by a net curtain.

● RIGHT Colour plays an important part in giving a feeling of fun. The primary colours here convey excitement, aided by the boy's red sweater.

● ABOVE Look for different angles when photographing children. Looking down on this small girl has increased the sense of her diminutive size. The picture was lit with a flash attachment on the camera's hot shoe.

● LEFT When photographing children (or anyone) out of doors in bright sunlight look out for harsh shadows. Make sure the background does not dominate the picture, and is not ugly or uninteresting.

OLDER CHILDREN

Younger children can soon get bored and restless when being photographed, but older children can be awkward in front of the camera from the start — especially when in their early teens. It is often better to photograph older children in a group rather than singly. Having a friend along to support them will give them confidence.

If a teenage girl is being photographed she will probably have quite definite views on how she wants to look. Discuss what she wants to wear and the sort of make-up she wants, if any.

When shooting indoors, decide on the background. Will it be in the subject's room with a background of posters, or is it possible to rig up a small home studio?

When shooting out of doors in bright sun, watch for shadows on the face and use fill-in flash where necessary. Backlighting can be used to create a more romantic feel. Try using a reflector to throw light back onto the face.

When older boys are being photographed, they may feel more comfortable if they are pursuing one of their hobbies. You could take pictures of them making a model or working on a bike. If they play a musical instrument, this might be included as a useful prop.

With boys and girls alike, take care not to talk down to them or patronize them. This will create a bad atmosphere from the start. Ask what their interests are and talk to them on equal terms.

With groups of older children it is often difficult to get them all to do the right thing at once. Try to position them to ensure that no one obscures anyone else.

Experiment with different angles and lenses, and do not be afraid to bend a few rules. The result can certainly repay the trouble.

● ABOVE These children were on holiday. The older ones kept teasing one another, but eventually they got themselves together and formed this group. Care was taken to make sure that no one covered anyone else.

● RIGHT This picture of a teenage girl was taken using available light coming through her bedroom window. Photographing her in familiar surroundings made her feel relaxed and at ease from the start. The posters on the wall behind her were put out of focus so as not to distract from her, and the camera was focused on her eyes.

● LEFT The picture was taken in the two girls' room. It is one of a series of shots that were taken of them dressing up. This gave them something to do between shots, and allowed them to contribute their own ideas about how they wanted to be photographed. It is important to deal with older children on equal terms.

GROUPS

Very often when photographing groups of people there is always someone looking the wrong way, keeping their eyes shut or making a silly gesture or face. As a photographer it will take all your expertise as a director to get everyone to do what you want them to do when you want them to do it. The knack is to strike a happy medium between a jovial atmosphere and firmness. Of course not all groups of people that you photograph are going to be under your control. If this is the case it is then up to you to find the right angle and be ready for the right moment. You will need to get yourself into a position where the light is at its best.

It might be advantageous in certain circumstances to photograph people

● LEFT By including the overhanging foliage from the tree in the foreground a natural frame to the picture has been achieved. The people listening to the band have also added foreground interest. These details help to draw the eye to the main centre of interest, the group of bandsmen playing under the canopy of the bandstand.

● LEFT This shot was taken in a steam bath in Moscow. The attendants were only too willing to pose for the photograph and directing them to the required positions was quite easy. The lighting was a combination of flash and available light. The camera was mounted on a tripod and the shutter fired with a cable release. This meant that it was easier to keep an eye on the attendants' gestures and expressions and to direct them to adopt the pose required. Because of the style of the building – it looks more like a gothic church than a steam bath – a certain incongruity has been achieved.

unaware, but then if they discover what you are up to they may get annoyed or move away. Often if a group of people know they are being photographed they will play for the camera and probably agree to your requests. If you are shooting indoors the chances are you will be able to direct people to adopt the positions you want. Take a good look at their characteristics. Decide who is the most interesting so that they can be in the foreground or other prominent position.

If there are many people to fit into the group, position them or take a viewpoint so that no one is obscured by anyone else. Consider whether some would be better sitting while others stand. It would be an advantage to work with the camera on a tripod and use a cable release. In this case you can position everyone to your liking. Also, when it comes to taking the actual shot, you can keep an eye on the group better from the camera viewpoint than looking through the viewfinder all the time. If you do use this method and your camera is set to auto exposure you will have to cover the viewfinder. On nearly all cameras there is a small button that brings a shield over the viewfinder. This cuts out light entering the eyepiece which would affect the camera metering mechanism and result in underexposure.

● RIGHT These men were playing cards on a terrace that was overlooked by a car park. It was a matter of chance that they were seen from this angle but full advantage has been taken of the viewpoint. Although the players became aware that they were being photographed they were too absorbed in their game to care. With a large group like this invariably someone will be looking the wrong way or making an unwanted gesture. Since it was not possible to direct them, several shots were taken so that a selection could be made.

● LEFT These five men were photographed at a barbecue being held at a ranch in Arizona. Either because of what they were drinking or because they were naturally confident, they had no inhibitions when it came to having their picture taken. Always be on the lookout for spontaneous situations but take care that unwanted details are cropped out of your shots.

Taking pictures of older people can be very rewarding for the creative photographer. Often they will have aged in a way which reflects their working life. For instance, a person with an outdoor occupation is likely to have a tanned, lined face – unlike an office worker. It is these physical characteristics that make such photographs so interesting.

At the same time, the photographer should show some sensitivity toward someone who is no longer young, not just in the way they are portrayed but also in the effect that a long photographic session, or even the use of flash, might have on them. If someone is a real character but frail, try several short sessions, and if possible use available light.

Older people are not only interesting in their own right but may well be surrounded by items collected over a lifetime, or they may be dressed in a way that reflects their life, as in the case of the Chelsea Pensioner shown here.

A serious approach may be required to illustrate inadequate living conditions or illness. But if it is not, look for humour in pictures. This is not the same as being humiliating or patronizing. An easy way to photograph an older person might be to strike up a conversation with them. If so, be patient and do not give the impression that they are repetitive or long winded.

Look for different viewpoints, or go in close and concentrate on a particular area such as hands. Black and white photography may be better than colour, since it allows greater expression and more evocative images.

● ABOVE These two men were photographed outside a café in Italy. They had no inhibitions about having their pictures taken, so that several angles could be explored. They were delighted with an instant Polaroid picture, which made them more receptive to being photographed. A medium telephoto lens, 100 mm, put the background slightly out of focus, drawing attention to their faces.

● LEFT The picture was taken from a high viewpoint, as the room was rather small and as much of it as possible was required for the photograph. The woman is Frances Partridge, the oldest surviving member of the Bloomsbury Group. She is surrounded by reminders of the group, including a portrait of Lytton Strachey.

● ABOVE Many older people wear clothes that symbolize their way of life, such as this Chelsea Pensioner. His hat and red coat add picturesque colour. His face is full of character and is lit by hazy sunlight. If the subject of the shot wears glasses, care should be taken with reflections, especially when using flash.

● RIGHT Always be on the look-out for a humorous shot, but do not try to make fun of older people in a humiliating way. Most people have a sense of humour and will see the amusing side of a picture that tells a good story.

CANDID SHOTS

• BELOW This is an example of being prepared for a spontaneous shot. The woman bending over the child makes the obvious comment on 'little and large'. However, the picture is taken in such a way that the woman's face is hidden, so she remains anonymous and not humiliated. The shot was taken using a 300 mm lens that kept a good distance between the woman and the camera.

Candid photography is when people are photographed in a natural or unposed way and may be unaware of the camera. Being prepared is essential – carry a camera at all times and have it ready for use. Since the opportunity for shots may occur when the light is low and there is no time for flash, or when flash might be intrusive, try a medium-fast film such as 200 or 400 ISO.

If you do take a photograph quickly and the subject is still in position, see if you can shoot from a different viewpoint that may be better. Even if the person moves away altogether you will still have that important first shot, but chances for improvement are usually available. Perhaps the best lens to use would be a 80–300 mm zoom lens. This means that the picture can be framed in such a way as to crop out any unwanted detail. It also means that you can get in close to the subject from some distance away without having to change lenses. In this way you can work unnoticed without inhibiting the person or people and ruining the spontaneity of the situation. In candid photography it is often the look, gesture or position of a person that makes the shot.

It is an advantage to have TTL metering, preferably with spot metering facilities. This means a reading can be taken from the subject's face and you can expose for the skin tone. If the person is against a white wall or bright reflective background then there is the risk of underexposure if the meter takes an average reading; this is because the background would be giving off the most light.

• LEFT This elderly man was quietly reading his book. After the initial photograph was taken another viewpoint was found. This made a better composition with the row of flower pots and added interest to his surroundings. Never think you have captured the perfect shot until you have exhausted all the possibilities.

● LEFT At first glance this picture looks like a man reading a newspaper but it is in fact a dummy. This plays a trick on the viewer and creates another dimension to candid photography.

● ABOVE Is it the unexpectedness of seeing a priest gambling that makes this candid picture a success? He was absorbed in selecting the winner in the next race and was oblivious to having his picture taken even though he was quite close to the camera.

● ABOVE Having had just a little too much to drink, this man fell asleep on the bonnet of his car. Shots like this abound for the alert photographer.

● RIGHT Even when people appear to be unaware of having their photograph taken, a second glance may contradict this. This boy in a Tunisian market appears to be asleep but a careful look shows that he is in fact watching from the corner of half-closed eyes.

GOING IN CLOSE

Pictures of people do not all have to be head and shoulders or full length. There are many other areas of the body that lend themselves to being photographed. Some of these pictures can be evocative and sensual. Others can be character studies, such as shots of gnarled hands and wrinkled skin.

Most standard lenses will not focus close enough, and a close-up attachment of some kind will be needed: extension rings, bellows or a macro lens. Close-up lenses that fit onto the front of an existing lens like a filter are available, but the quality of the image is not very good. Some telephoto lenses can also be focused to quite short distances and will give excellent close-up shots. With all these devices depth of field is very limited.

For close-up work the camera has to be kept perfectly still and it is advisable to use a tripod. In particular, extension tubes and bellows reduce the amount of light passing through the lens, so that exposures have to be long. They are made even longer by the need to use a small aperture to make the most of the available depth of field. When using available light, and with the lens stopped down to f22 or even f32, an exposure of 1 second or more may be needed. The subject also has to be kept still, which can be difficult.

If lighting a close-up picture with flash, be careful of shadows. What looks acceptable from a distance may be harsh and ugly in close-up and dominate the picture. As the camera will be only a short way from the subject, it is vital to ensure that it does not cast its own shadow onto the area.

Once the photographs have been developed, consider making enlarged prints. These could become many times larger than life size, with a strikingly abstract, sculptural quality.

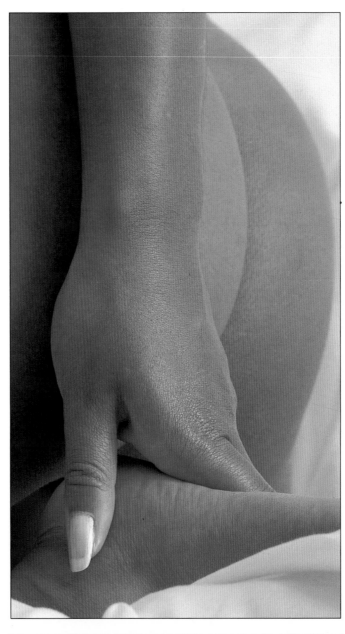

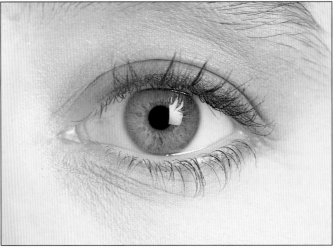

● RIGHT This picture was taken with a macro lens. The subject's feet were surrounded with a white sheet so that they became isolated and dominated the picture. They were lit with flash, using a 'softbox' to diffuse the light. The angle of view gives a sculptural effect.

● LEFT Going in close on this girl's hand, with her own body as the background, has created a sensual picture. A 100 mm lens focused at its nearest distance was used – this shows that close-ups are possible without special lenses or accessories.

● LEFT This picture was taken using a combination of extension rings and macro lens. The girl's eye was approximately 5 cm (2 in) from the front of the lens. It was essential to mount the lens on a tripod and to have a support for the girl's head. The picture was lit by flash and the depth of field, even at f22, was virtually non-existent.

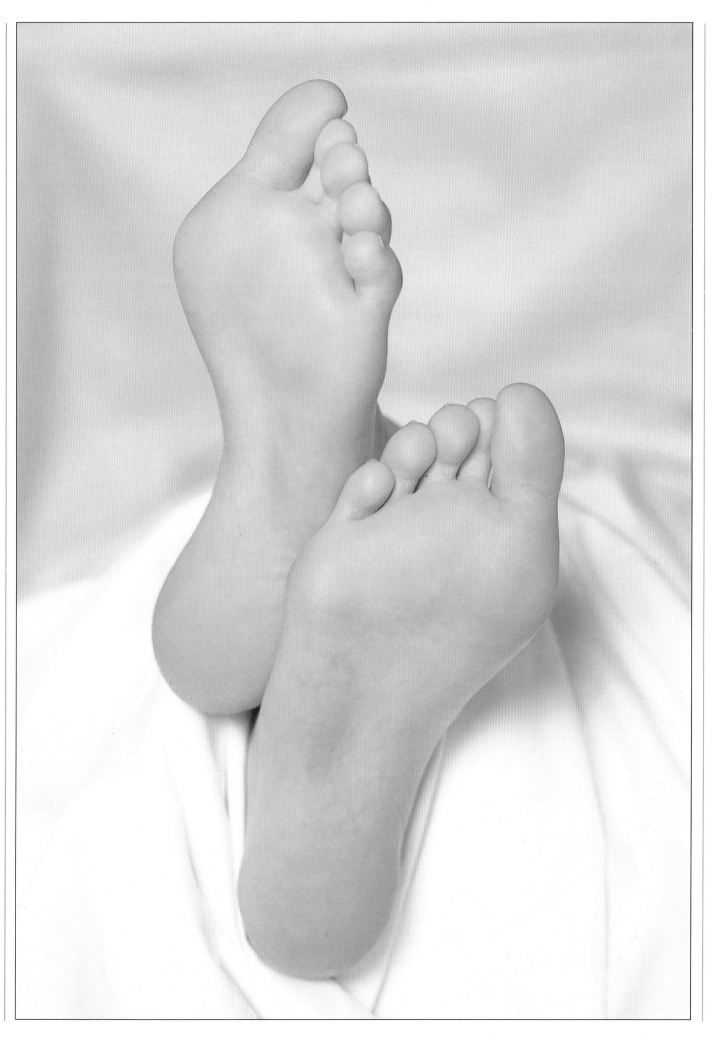

High-key pictures are those where the tonal range is predominantly light. These are not to be confused with high-contrast pictures, which are images that have extremes of tone with few if any mid-tones. In contrast, low-key pictures have a tonal range mainly from the dark end of the scale. Again, these are not the same as low-contrast pictures, which are images which have a narrow range of tone – this is probably due to underexposure, and the prints will have a muddy look.

When a full tonal range is easy to achieve, why, then, take high- or low-key pictures?

High-key pictures can look very romantic, and sometimes achieve an ethereal quality. If the background to a picture is uninteresting or intrusive it may be possible to fade it out by overexposing it. This may cause flare around the subject but, handled carefully, even this can be used to

● LEFT This low-key picture was taken in a studio, using just one light. This was placed to the side of, and slightly behind, the model. A reflector to the left and just in front of him bounced back just enough light to give detail in his face. The smoke from the cigarette shows up because it is backlit. If the light had been at the front the smoke would not have been visible.

• ABOVE Although this young girl is wearing a medium coloured top the majority of the tones are from the lighter end of the scale. Her hair, backlit by the sun, adds to the high-key nature of the picture. A reflector was used to throw light back onto her face.

creative advantage. High-key pictures can also portray freshness, a virginal quality, or the innocence of the newborn.

Conversely, low-key pictures can convey isolation or loneliness. They can be very atmospheric.

The easiest way to create low-key effects in the studio is with what is known as a 'rim light'. The light is positioned slightly behind the subject. This creates a slight halo effect on the side the light is coming from. Using a reflector or a fill-in light can give the shaded side of the face just enough tone. The result is an image with dark tones, but one in which the subject is easily discernible.

• LEFT This baby was photographed on a continuous roll of white background paper so that there is no line at the junction of the floor and wall. A large 'softbox' light was used, and this has created a very high-key picture.

BLACK AND WHITE PORTRAITS ON LOCATION

Photographing people out of doors or in their homes in black and white can give strong and incisive images. Unlike photographing in a studio, however, there is not full control of lighting.

When using available light, some thought is needed to make the lighting work. When a flashgun or a portable flash unit is used, the light can be put where it is needed. If bright sunlight is causing shadows on the person's face, there are several choices. One is to move the person to an area of shadow where the light is more even. Another is to use fill-in flash to soften the shadows.

If shooting against the light, a reflector can be used to bounce light back onto the subject's face. If, on the other hand, it seems that a silhouette

would make an evocative image, take the exposure reading from the light behind the subject.

When working out of doors, even if the light is bright, it can be interesting to use a film faster than would normally be chosen. This will give increased contrast and grain, even a 'gritty' look, as the picture of the youths shows.

Always look for a new angle, especially when photographing groups of people. There is nothing duller than a straight line of people rigidly sitting or standing. Keep watch for an unexpected chance, and always have the camera loaded and ready.

Remember that, unlike colour film, black and white is not affected by differences in light sources. Whether shooting in tungsten or fluorescent light or daylight, only the intensity of the light need be considered.

● LEFT When out and about, always be on the look-out for an unusual or spontaneous portrait, such as this one of a boy hiding behind his balloon. A camera loaded and at the ready allows the alert photographer to seize such moments.

● RIGHT Asking these five young girls to lie on the ground and look up at the camera has given a picture with a most unusual viewpoint. Do not be afraid to look for unconventional angles. This shot might have worked equally well if the photographer had lain on the ground and looked up at them.

● LEFT Background can say a lot about the person in a portrait. Here it gives just enough of a clue to show that he is a fisherman. Black and white has worked well here to give a 'gritty' appearance to the picture.

● ABOVE Silhouettes make a striking effect. This brother and sister were photographed in the entrance to a cave. Exposing for the background has made the figures underexposed, and also the cave itself, which makes an attractive frame.

● LEFT These youths were allowed to position themselves as they wanted. A fast film, 1600 ISO, has given a grainy effect which suits their rather menacing air.

With black and white as with colour, photographing people in a studio gives total control over the lighting. For black and white film, look for lighting that gives a good tonal range, or an unusual directional light that will give a striking effect.

Getting the right exposure is just as important with black and white as it is with colour, but when making prints in the darkroom there is far more latitude for altering the final image. 'Shading' and 'dodging' – that is, holding back shadows or underexposed areas of the negative, and selectively printing up highlighted or overexposed areas of the negative – can be done when making a print with an enlarger.

Before taking any pictures in a studio try to work out the effect that is wanted. This will inspire confidence in the sitter. They will be put at ease if they see the lights and equipment being handled in a confident manner.

● ABOVE Rolls of studio background paper are available from professional photographic stores. These are a standard 3 m wide × 11 m long (10 ft × 36 ft), and come in many colours. When suspended from a wall or ceiling they can be extended along the floor. This creates a seamless backdrop on which to position the subject.

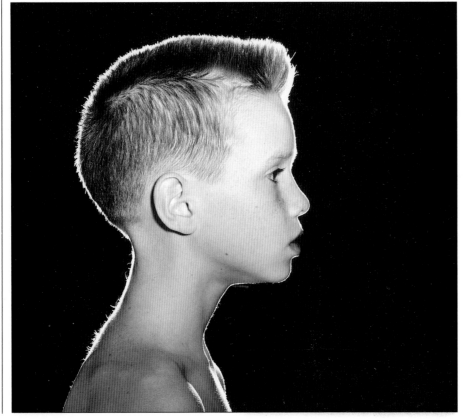

● LEFT A light was placed directly behind the young boy and pointing straight at him. The light was fitted with a 'snoot', which has narrowed the beam down to create the bright outline around his head. A weak directional light was used to illuminate his face. The picture was taken against a black backdrop.

• TOP LEFT Taking portraits in the studio allows complete control over lighting and composition. The possibilities are endless, as these three pictures show. Here the group is arranged to give prominence to the leader. The main light is coming from the right, but a weaker fill-in light has been put at the left. This arrangement shows some modelling in their faces. If the two lights had been of the same strength, ugly cross shadows would have occurred and their features would have looked flat.

• CENTRE LEFT Placing the main light directly in front of and below the group, shining upwards, gives an eerie effect. When positioning lights in a studio always return to the camera viewpoint to check the result.

• BOTTOM LEFT Standing on some steps and looking down on the group gives another angle. Whether photographing groups or individuals, always look for new viewpoints and lighting effects. The possibilities are limitless.

LEARNING TO USE LIGHTS

Explore the effect that one light can have on someone's face. If it is placed at an angle of 45 degrees to their face, set medium-high so that the shadow falls between the nose and half-way down the upper lip: the effect will be reasonably natural. If the light is straight in front and higher, there will be heavy shadows under the eyes, nose and chin. A light set below the face pointing upward will give a ghostly look. Practice, and a keen eye for where shadows fall, will soon make it easy to achieve a desired style. Once the basics have been mastered, all that is needed is a little imagination.

POLAROID MONTAGE

Polaroid film gives good instant portraits, but it is worth trying something different, such as making a montage portrait of several Polaroid prints stuck together. This technique was made famous by the artist David Hockney, who has exhibited works in this medium in major art galleries worldwide.

Making Polaroid montages is more than just a way of constructing an interesting image. It is a good exercise in looking and seeing. Consider having a conversation with someone. During this time one is aware that every part of the person is there, but at any one moment the eye is focused on only a single part. Moving one's gaze from the face to the feet gives a completely differently framed picture. You remain aware that the head is still there, but it is out of focus, as if it formed part of the background, and is not being concentrated on. Now compare a full-length portrait of that person. Every part is there and in focus, but it is not what the eye saw during the conversation. Even if it is a fine photograph it lacks something vital.

However, by building up a picture of that person from a series of quick Polaroid snaps, an image can be made that is like a series of glances. There is no attempt to make a smoothly connected picture where every part fits perfectly together. The assembled picture shows that there are ways of seeing that are more truthful to actual experience than a normal portrait. It reflects the way people actually see.

● ABOVE Not all the small pictures in this portrait align perfectly, but this makes the viewer look all the more closely at the girl's features. When the portrait is viewed as a whole, certain pictures in it may seem to jar and upset the conventional form of a close-up portrait. But think of talking to someone, perhaps across a dinner table. Visual emphasis changes throughout the conversation: one moment one is looking at their eyes, the next their mouth, or at a mole not previously noticed. The world is viewed not as a whole, but as a series of bits of information.

● LEFT At first glance this might look like a standard picture of someone sitting on a sofa, cut up and stuck together in a grid of rectangles. But a closer look reveals that each picture in the grid is taken from a slightly different viewpoint. For instance, the carpet and the things on it are seen from above. Ordinarily, a viewer standing in front of the sofa would be aware of the floor while looking at the person, or at the picture above her. But to see the floor clearly it would be necessary to look downward and look at it from a different viewpoint, which is the one shown here.

EDITING YOUR PICTURES

Once you have got your pictures back from the processing laboratory the next step is to edit them. How often you must have visited friends and been subjected to all their holiday snaps, with comments like, 'You can just see part of that church we told you about in the background,' or, 'This is a bit blurred but you can recognize John.' Not all their pictures may be like that, but they have not given enough thought to weeding out the unsuccessful or uninteresting ones. Even good pictures will make little impact if they are submerged in a flood of bad shots.

Look at any magazine and consider the pictures that have been used. In a photo spread the few pictures that have been printed will have been chosen from several rolls of film. In a newspaper or news magazine, pictures of an event may have been chosen not just from many rolls but from the work of several photographers.

When looking through your pictures, discard those that are badly exposed. Next, look at subjects of which you have taken more than one shot. Select one or two that give a good overall view. If there are others where you have gone in close, choose the ones that give the most interesting details. After this initial editing, decide whether any pictures would be improved by being cropped or differently framed when reprinted.

It is quite easy to select the best of a series of holiday pictures, but greater care is needed for a series of portraits or other studio pictures. These will have been taken in controlled conditions and will probably all be technically sound. Here you must look for the frames that show the model in the most flattering or arresting way.

It may seem wasteful to discard so many pictures, but the results will be that people actually look forward to seeing your pictures, and people you have photographed will be pleased with being seen at their best.

● ABOVE This frame has been printed virtually full frame. It was chosen in the initial selection to show an enlargement from a high viewpoint.

● RIGHT The printer was asked to angle the masking on the enlarger baseboard so that the model appears at a very slight angle.

● ABOVE RIGHT For this picture the printer was asked to crop in tight on the model. When having prints made at a professional laboratory it is a good idea to see if you can discuss your requirements with the printer beforehand.

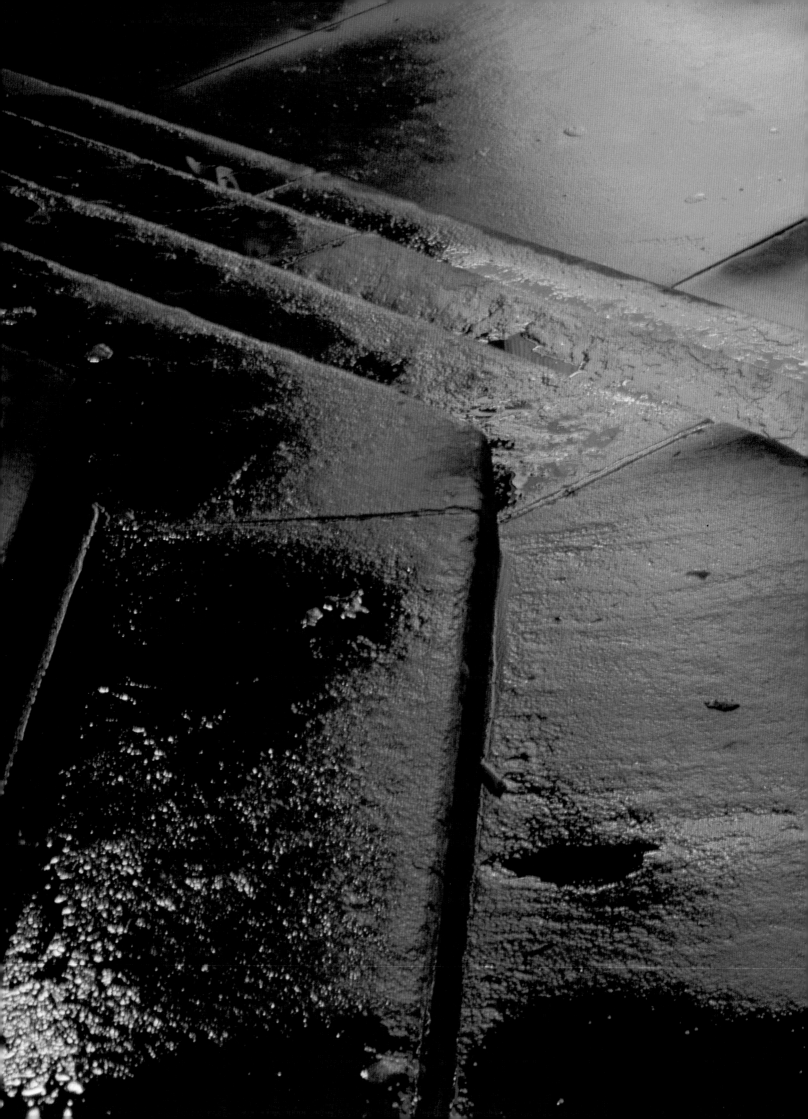

Improving Your Technique

INTRODUCTION

Once the photographer gains confidence, the opportunities for improvement and experimentation are numerous. The methods of enhancing images are immensely varied and exciting: they range from the simple addition of a special effect filter or a specialized lens, or the more complicated manipulation of films and prints. The photographic techniques used to achieve original and extraordinary effects are available to everyone; do not be afraid of experimentation – it can produce some stunning shots.

PRESENTATION

When your pictures are processed and you have edited them you will want to decide how best to present them.

PRINTS

If the shots were made on negative film you will have prints. Many types of album are available: traditional ones where the prints are fixed to the leaves with corner mounts, and more modern kinds where the pictures are held in individual sheaths which are flipped over to view them.

For special photographs that you have cropped and had enlarged, and perhaps toned, there are folio books. These are spiral bound and come in various sizes. The prints are mounted on card and slid into transparent sleeves. When the book is opened the prints lie flat. This makes a very professional presentation. An alternative to this is to have your prints laminated. They are encapsulated between two layers of plastic – clear on the image side and black on the back – which are heat sealed. The prints can then be put individually into a folio case. The virtue of this method is that it can accommodate prints of different sizes.

TRANSPARENCIES

These can be made into prints, but there are other ways of presenting them. There are black masks that hold a single transparency, and which are slid into a clear plastic sleeve which protects them. These mounts are made for transparency sizes from 35 mm to 10 × 8 in. Mounts for pictures from 35 mm to 6 × 7 in can have the same overall size, and can be filed in a custom-made drawer for the best protection and access.

As well as individual mounts there are types that hold transparencies in groups. Typical mounts of this kind would hold 35 mm in groups of 24, or 5 × 4 in

transparencies in groups of 4. In all these cases the mounted transparencies have to be viewed on a light box.

Transparencies can also be made into slides, mounted in stiff holders, for projection. For the more advanced projectors the slides are put into magazines, which protect them and can be used as permanent boxes. Magazines may be straight or circular. The projector has a mechanism for picking out one slide at a time and projecting it; some machines have a remote control. For a really professional presentation two or more projectors can be synchronized and combined with a soundtrack or commentary or music, or both. Some shows use as many as 60 projectors, programmed with a soundtrack by means of a computer. These displays, which are known under

the general heading of AV (audio-visual), can be quite stunning.

A new way of viewing your photographs is to have them transferred to CD-ROM. They are recorded onto what looks like a CD, though it needs a special player which is connected to your television in the same way as a video recorder. At present each disc holds about 100 images. They can be viewed in any sequence, and a soundtrack is included on the disc. You can zoom into an interesting part of the image, pan from side to side and move up and down. A suitably equipped photographic dealer can make prints of any pictures on the disc. The scope for this system is enormous. You can have

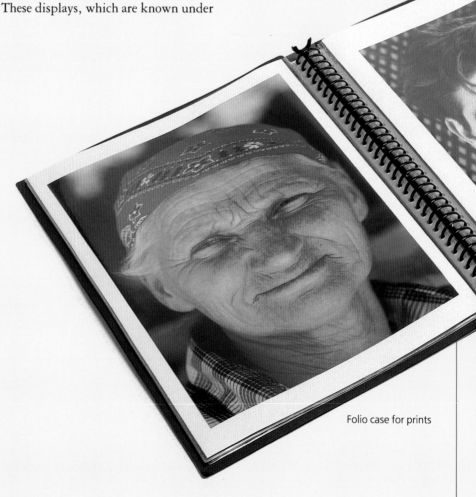

Folio case for prints

images transferred from several existing discs to a single new one to make a record, say, of your children growing up. This may seem a startling advance, but when you recall that twenty years ago most people had not even heard of video you will appreciate how quickly new technology becomes the norm.

Projector

35 mm slide tray

Plastic 35 mm
transparency mounts

Light box

Card transparency
mounting masks

Special films can be used not only for their normal purpose, but also to enlarge a photographer's creative scope.

For example, tungsten-balanced film used in daylight gives pictures a predominantly blue cast. In some cases this can give a nightime look to a picture, or, if the film is slightly overexposed, a hard, slightly bleached look – this is often seen in fashion photography. Using daylight-balanced colour film in tungsten light gives results with a predominantly orange cast. This too can be exploited creatively, especially when the film is slightly overexposed. In either case, be imaginative and prepared to experiment with new effects.

Infrared film gives strangely coloured pictures. Black and white infrared film gives a night effect even on pictures taken in daylight. The results can be unpredictable, and some trial and error is needed to get good results – though there is always the possibility of getting a striking effect by accident. Processing infrared film can be a problem, since the chemical process required is the type known as E4. All ordinary laboratories now use a process called E6. It can be difficult to track down a laboratory with facilities for the older process. One of the main uses of infrared film is in medical photo-graphy, and the photographic laboratory of a large hospital may be able to advise you.

Very fast film can also be used to give special effects. It gives very grainy, high-contrast pictures, and if it is uprated the effect is exaggerated. 1600 ISO black and white film can be uprated to 3400 or even higher.

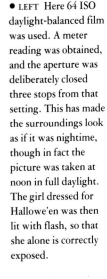

● LEFT Here 64 ISO daylight-balanced film was used. A meter reading was obtained, and the aperture was deliberately closed three stops from that setting. This has made the surroundings look as if it was nightime, though in fact the picture was taken at noon in full daylight. The girl dressed for Hallowe'en was then lit with flash, so that she alone is correctly exposed.

● RIGHT The same idea is carried a stage further. This picture was also taken in full daylight; 50 ISO tungsten-balanced film was used, under-exposed by two stops, which has made the sky deep blue. To both expose and light the girl correctly, a flash unit was used with an 85B filter placed over it instead of over the lens.

● LEFT Infrared film can produce un-expected results, and a certain amount of experimentation is required. The leaves of the trees and the grass appear magenta. At a different time of day or with a different light source the results would have been quite different.

● BELOW Using 1600 film rated at 3400 ISO has produced a very grainy but effective portrait. This shot was taken with available light from a window. Of course, if a film is uprated it is necessary to tell the processing laboratory that this has been done and what the increase is, so that the lab can adjust the processing time accordingly.

SHIFT LENSES

A shift lens, also called a perspective control (PC) lens, is a great addition to the photographer's equipment, and especially useful for architectural photography. With a 5 × 4 camera it is possible to move the front panel, on which the lens is mounted, up and down and from side to side, or to swing it vertically or tilt it horizontally. For 35 mm SLR and some medium format cameras there are lenses that can be moved up and down or across, and some lenses have a tilt facility as well. In the 35 mm range these lenses usually have a focal length of 28 or 35 mm.

When using one of these lenses to photograph a tall building, instead of tilting the camera up to fit in the whole building, the camera can be kept pointing straight ahead and the axis of the lens is shifted relative to the film plane – that is, the lens is moved upward but kept parallel to the film. This movement is known as a shift. The whole building now appears in the picture, but with a difference. With a normal lens and the camera angled up, the vertical lines of the building will converge towards the top of the frame. With a shift lens, as long as the camera is kept horizontal, all verticals in the picture will appear vertical and there will be no convergence, even when the lens is shifted as far as it can go.

Even when photographing things that are less strongly vertical, distortion can still be caused by angling the camera to cut out unwanted features such as an untidy foreground. Here, keeping the camera level and using a shift lens can eliminate unwanted areas at the bottom, top, left or right of the frame without causing distortion.

Before deciding to buy a shift lens, it is a good idea to hire one from a professional photography store and try out its effects.

● ABOVE To keep all the columns vertical in this shot of the Banqueting House in London, the camera had to be kept level. With a normal lens this would have cut out the wonderful ceiling painted by Rubens, and would have included a lot of the comparatively dull floor. Using the shift lens to its maximum has cut out much of the floor and brought in the ceiling.

● RIGHT A problem with photographing objects with shiny reflective surfaces, such as cars, is that the camera and photographer can appear in them. The effect can be corrected by standing to one side of the car, but by using the horizontal shift movement of the lens the car can be brought into the centre of the frame without the photographer or the camera appearing as a reflection.

• Using a conventional lens, the camera had to be tilted upward to fit the whole building into the frame. The vertical lines converge so that the building seems to be leaning.

• To keep the verticals straight the plane of the film must be parallel to the plane of the front of the building, which means that the camera body must be absolutely level. But here this results in the top of the tallest building being cut off.

• Here the camera is still level, but the shift lens has been moved upward. The whole building is now in view, but its sides are completely vertical. Also, a lot of uninteresting foreground detail has been cropped out of the picture.

FISHEYE LENSES

Among all the lenses that are available the fisheye lens is low on most people's list of priorities. The uses of this lens are limited and it is rather expensive. Nevertheless, it can be highly effective in the right situation.

It is sensible to hire a fisheye lens from a professional photographic dealer and try it out before deciding to buy one. If there seem to be many genuinely worthwhile uses for it, then and only then consider a purchase.

Most people looking through an SLR camera with a fisheye lens for the first time find it highly amusing to see the world through a 180-degree angle of vision. Objects appear severely distorted, and it is easy to get carried away by gimmicky shots of people's faces close to the lens, but used thoughtfully, a fisheye lens can produce uniquely striking images. The art of exploiting the lens is to make the photograph look as if a fisheye lens has not been used at all. Great care is needed in choosing a viewpoint and in framing the subject to obtain the best effect.

Because of their extremely wide angle of view, fisheye lenses cannot be used with lens hoods. Filters can be fitted, but these are special ones that are screwed in at the back of the lens. Graduated filters cannot be used.

There is a difficulty when using flash. Even when a flash gun is fitted with a wide angle attachment, the area that it illuminates is no wider than the field of view of a 28 mm lens. This falls far short of what is needed for a fisheye. If flash has to be used, at least two, even three or four flash heads are needed.

● ABOVE This hallway ceiling needed to be lit with flash, and four flash heads were necessary to give the required coverage. The symmetry of the design has created an interesting architectural conundrum.

● BELOW Like the domed British Museum Reading Room, the Olympic cycle track in Moscow lends itself well to being photographed with a fisheye lens. The banked curves at both ends look much as might be expected, and not unduly distorted. The ceiling panels add to a strong feeling of perspective.

● ABOVE A good example of how to use a fisheye lens without the result looking gimmicky. The Reading Room of the British Museum has a domed ceiling and the reading desks radiate out from the centre of the floor. Keeping the camera level allows the beautiful dome to be seen in its entirety, as well as including the floor in the shot. The curved lines of the room harmonize with the distortion caused by the lens, so that the shot looks as if it had been taken with a normal wide angle lens.

● LEFT Taken from the dome of the cathedral in Florence, Italy, this fisheye shot gives a striking panoramic view. The inclusion of the dome itself in the foreground leads the eye into the maze of streets below, and out into the Tuscan countryside beyond.

ZOOM LENSES

Zoom lenses allow the use of a continuous range of focal lengths without having to change lenses. If two zoom lenses are used, it is possible with only one change to go from 28 mm wide angle to 300 mm telephoto. The image quality is not quite as good as that of a prime lens, but the slight difference will be apparent only to the most critical viewer.

Many zoom lenses can now be used with autofocus systems, but some of these cannot take certain filter holders. It is as well to make sure what will fit before a problem arises.

As well as taking conventional pictures at any chosen focal length, a zoom lens can also be 'zoomed' during the exposure to create an interesting effect. This should be done during a moderately long exposure, say ⅛ second, to make the movement apparent. There will be a pattern of streaks radiating from the centre of the frame. Zooming from wide angle to telephoto will create a different effect from going the other way. The most effective shots with this technique are those which have strong highlights or colours which will make a noticeable pattern. This gives a feeling of movement, as if the objects are flying straight out of the frame. The slow shutter speed will require the camera to be mounted on a tripod. It may take a little practice to perfect the technique, but passable results should be achieved quite quickly. Like all special effects, this should not be over-used.

● ABOVE Here is a conventional view of a boy standing astride his bike. He is deliberately placed in front of a strongly coloured backdrop.

● ABOVE Here, he is in the same position, but this time a shutter speed of ⅛ second was chosen, and during the exposure the lens was zoomed half-way through its range of focal length. This created strong radiating lines of colour and gives a sense of speed.

● RIGHT The boy is still in the same position, but the lens has been moved from 80 mm to 300 mm. It looks as if he is going round a corner at speed.

● ABOVE Neon lights make a good subject for zooming. Here is the conventional view . . .

● LEFT . . . and here is the effect with the zoom.

USING A MACRO LENS

Additional equipment may not be absolutely necessary, but it can offer new photographic possibilities. One of the most useful accessories is some means of taking close-up shots. There are several ways of doing this.

The cheapest is a close-up lens which is fitted over the normal camera lens. This does not, however, give a very high-quality image. When using such a lens on an SLR camera, focusing and framing are relatively easy, but when it is fitted to a camera with a viewfinder the distance to the subject must be measured. The lens will come with instructions about the correction to make to the focus setting. Because the viewfinder is offset, an educated guess will have to be made about how to point the camera.

For some SLR cameras it is possible to buy a reversing ring. This allows the lens to be mounted back to front, which makes it possible to focus on closer objects. The lens is not designed to be used backwards, so the image will not be of the best quality.

The only really satisfactory methods are to use extension rings or bellows, or to buy a separate macro lens. The rings or bellows are fixed to the camera as a lens would be, and the lens is attached to the front. Extension rings usually come in sets of three, and can be used singly or together. When using them with certain lenses 1:1 magnification can be obtained, which means that the image is the same size as the object. Bellows work in the same way, but can be moved smoothly in and out so that any degree of magnification within their range can be obtained.

A macro lens allows close-up work without having to fuss with these awkward devices. However, some macro lenses can be used with rings or bellows to give even greater magnification.

● ABOVE The two small leaves were photographed with a macro lens and extension rings. The magnification on the original film was 1:1, life-size. A soft focus filter was used on the lens and the leaves were lit by electronic flash with a very soft diffuser. When working at such high magnifications exposure time has to be increased considerably.

● LEFT This picture was taken with a macro lens at almost full magnification. A problem with any close-up work is depth of field, which at very high magnification is almost non-existent, as the picture shows. The nails are 6 cm (2½ in) long and quite thin, but when they are perfectly in focus the background, a mere 3 mm (⅛ in) away, is blurred.

● BELOW The section of lemon was photographed on a blue plate. The glaze is out of focus even though a tiny aperture of f45 was used, because the depth of field is so shallow. The high magnification and small aperture called for a very long exposure. The camera will always need to be mounted on a tripod, and it is advisable to use a cable release. If the camera has a mirror-up facility, operate this before firing the shutter, since even the slightest vibration caused by the mirror may blur the picture. It is also vital to make sure that the subject stays still.

SPECIAL FILTERS

Of all the accessories that are available, filters are the cheapest. Yet these simple attachments to the front of the lens – or sometimes to the rear – can radically alter the effect of a picture. There is a myriad of types to choose from. As with any camera accessory, you must pay attention to a few points in order to get a satisfying result.

Some filters cut down the amount of light entering the lens to such an extent that a longer exposure is needed. If your camera has TTL metering this will not be a problem, but with other cameras you will have to adjust exposure manually. Manufacturers of filters generally state the necessary amount of exposure adjustment: this is called the filter factor.

With a wide angle lens, vignetting may occur when a filter is put in front of the lens. This means that the corners of the frame are cut off, because the angle of view of the lens is so great that it takes in the filter holder ring. This usually happens only with lenses of 21 mm or wider.

It is possible to use more than one filter at a time, but do this only if it will enhance the image.

Some special effect filters, such as multiple image types, are fun but their use is strictly limited. Imagine looking at your holiday photographs and seeing them all as if through a kaleidoscope. You would quickly get bored. Even a graduated tobacco filter, which can help to lift a dull sky, would be tedious if all your pictures had this coloured sky.

● ABOVE A multiple image filter makes several tiger's heads appear. These filters come in different types, such as 2, 4 or 6 images. They can be used creatively but not too often.

● BELOW LEFT No filter has been used. BELOW RIGHT A soft focus filter has been added to diffuse the image.

● LEFT When this shot of Venice was taken the sky was rather grey and flat. A graduated tobacco filter has changed the colour of the sky, but the rest of the picture is unaffected. This is an effective filter but use it sparingly, or all your shots will look too alike.

● ABOVE An alternative to the tobacco filter is this pink graduated filter. Although this shot was taken at midday the filter, carefully used, makes it look like dawn.

● RIGHT A graduated neutral density filter will darken a sky without changing the colour. In this shot of Loch Torridon it has turned an already moody sky to a virtually night-time hue.

FILL-IN FLASH AND REFLECTORS

Often a photograph can be greatly enhanced by the use of a reflector or what is called fill-in flash. To many people it seems odd that you would use flash in bright sunlight but it helps by reducing unattractive shadows. Suppose it is a bright day and the sun is quite high. Imagine that the people you are going to photograph are facing the sun. This will cause them to have dark shadows under their eyes and nose. Even if they turn to one side the shadows might still remain, or if they move to a different location they may be in total shadow while the background beyond is bathed in sunshine. In either case the use of fill-in flash will eliminate the shadows or balance the foreground with the background, creating a better shot.

To do this take an exposure meter reading of the highlight area of the picture. Let us imagine it is $\frac{1}{125}$ second at f11. Set the camera to this exposure. If you are using an automatic flash gun set the aperture dial on it to f 5.6, in other words two stops less than the highlight exposure. If you are using a manual flash gun you will have to work out a combination of aperture and speed from the guide numbers of your flash gun to give you the appropriate exposure. The guide number tells you how strong a flash gun's power is and will alter depending on the speed of the film you are using. For example a film rated at 200 ISO will give a higher guide number than a film rated at 64 ISO.

From the flash gun manufacturer's instructions you can work out the correct aperture to use. Roughly speaking, this is calculated by dividing the guide number by the flash-to-subject distance. Having done this you are now ready to take your shot. The important point to remember is always to underexpose the flash. If you do not do this then the light from the flash will look too harsh and burn out all the shadow detail. Many photographers are nervous of using fill-in flash because they cannot see the effect it is having until the film is processed, unless of course they have the benefit of Polaroid.

With a reflector, on the other hand, you can see the effect immediately. You can buy custom-made reflectors in a variety of sizes and effects. These range from white and silver through to bronze and gold. Of course you might find yourself in a situation where you do not have a reflector and therefore will have to improvise. A piece of white card, a white sheet or a piece of aluminium foil will do. Let us imagine that the sun is behind your subject. If you hold the reflector so that the sun shines directly onto it you can bounce this light back

● FAR LEFT This picture was taken without the addition of flash.

● LEFT Here the aperture setting on the automatic flash gun was deliberately set at a wider opening than what was required for the available light. This resulted in a weak burst of flash that was just enough to eliminate the shadows under this young woman's eyes. If the same power had been used as for the available light then her face would have been burnt out and the final picture would have looked most unflattering.

to your subject. By changing your position and the angle of the reflector you can redirect the light to exactly where you need it. A silver reflector will give a harsher light than a white one, and a gold one will give a very warm effect. Many photographers prefer using a reflector to fill-in flash as they feel it gives a more natural light.

The use of a reflector or fill-in flash is not just restricted to photographing people. Perhaps you are going to photograph a table outdoors laid for lunch. The table is in the shade but, if you expose for it, then the house in the background, for example, will be overexposed. By using the flash to illuminate the table the two different exposures can be bought into line with one another. Whichever method you decide to use it is of course best to practise before you take some important photographs.

● LEFT These pictures illustrate the difference a reflector makes. In the top picture a white reflector has been used. Although this has bounced the required amount of light back into the subjects' faces it is rather cool. In the second picture a gold reflector makes the quality of the light warmer, giving a more pleasing effect.

● BELOW LEFT In this picture it was important to retain the detail of the house in the background. The exposure for this has meant that some of the items on the table and the owner of the vineyard are in shadow. By using fill-in flash, BELOW RIGHT, these shadows have been softened while still retaining detail. The result is a more pleasing balance between foreground and background.

SLOW SYNC FLASH

Flash used normally will freeze a moving object, and, if the exposure is correct, will evenly illuminate everything within its range. But, as in every aspect of photography, creative rule-breaking can produce stunning results; and this is particularly true of the unorthodox technique of slow sync flash.

Most 35 mm SLR cameras have a mark on the shutter speed dial that synchronizes the flash when the picture is taken. Usually this speed is $\frac{1}{60}$ or $\frac{1}{125}$ second. If a shutter speed faster than this is used the blinds of the focal plane shutter will not have time to open fully, so that part of the picture comes out unexposed. However, it is possible to use a lower speed such as $\frac{1}{15}$ or $\frac{1}{18}$ second and still synchronize the flash. The flash will not last any longer than usual, which means that it will be illuminating the scene for only part of the time the shutter is open.

If a slow shutter speed is used with flash to photograph a moving object when there is a reasonable amount of ambient light, the subject will be marked by a faint trail looking like 'speed lines' in cartoons. This can look very effective in an action shot such as the picture of a roller skater here.

The important thing is to use a shutter speed compatible with both the ambient light and the desired flash effect. For example, the film is 100 ISO; a meter reading of the ambient light says $\frac{1}{125}$ at f5.6. To get the slow sync effect a shutter speed of $\frac{1}{15}$ second is needed. To compensate for the difference the aperture should be reduced to f16. Set the dial on the flashgun to f16 or, if it is a manually controlled one, work out the flash-to-subject distance that normally requires an aperture of f16. The result should be worth the effort.

● ABOVE The young boy is almost frozen in mid-flight, even though the shutter speed used was only $\frac{1}{15}$ second. This is because he was lit mostly by the flash, not by ambient light. However, the daylight has had a curious effect on his outline so that it looks as if the sky were directly behind him. The ambient light needed a full stop more, but it was decided to underexpose for this to give the shot more impact. The boy's friends in the background complete the composition perfectly.

● RIGHT A similar technique was used indoors to photograph the baby. Here a shutter speed of $\frac{1}{8}$ second was used. The baby turned his head as the shot was taken and the flash fired. There was enough ambient light to let this movement show up. It has created an attractive background which increases the effectiveness of the portrait.

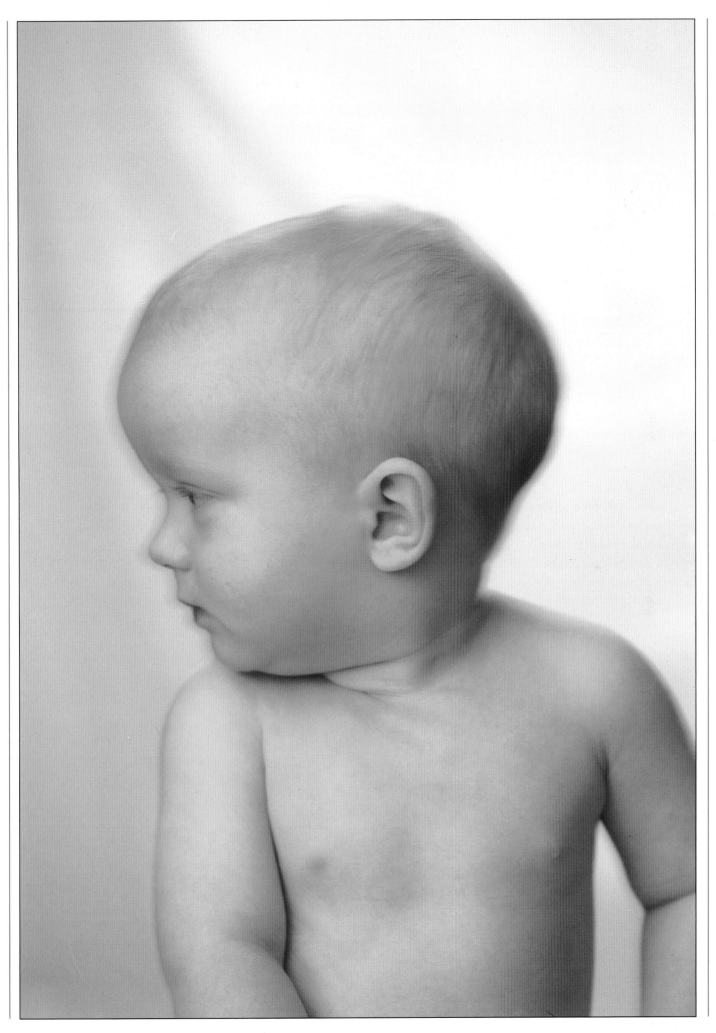

Instant photographs from Polaroid cameras have the obvious advantage over traditional media that the picture can be seen within seconds. But Polaroid film also lends itself to a wide variety of manipulations. Many of these need no more than the camera, the film, and a blunt-ended instrument such as a pen.

With Polaroid image film, for instance, as soon the picture is ejected from the camera the dyes inside the picture 'sandwich' can be squeezed around before they set. This will create bizarre patterns which can, with practice, be controlled quite precisely. When the picture appears fully the results are amazing.

A Polaroid back fitted to a conventional camera offers another technique, which is known as image transfer. Once the film has been exposed, it is pulled through a pair of rollers built into the back. These squeeze and spread the chemicals that develop the film. Development of a conventional print usually takes 90 seconds. But as soon as the film emerges it can be peeled off its backing sheet and this sheet pressed face downward onto a piece of paper throughly dampened with water, and left for the remainder of the development time. This transfers the image to the paper, after which the original material is discarded. The result has none of the smoothness of a conventional Polaroid print. The effect is raw and blurred, but often stunning.

Apart from Polaroid cameras and backs there is also the Polaroid transparency printer, which makes instant prints from conventional slides. These can be manipulated in the same way as those from a Polaroid back.

These are only some of the techniques. There are many others, including immersing the film in boiling water and scratching the emulsion.

● ABOVE This Polaroid camera picture was allowed to develop in the conventional way. The image is attractive but the background is rather boring.

● ABOVE Careful manipulation with a blunt pen of the dyes around the girl while the print was developing has created a much more interesting, almost abstract background.

● LEFT A variation of the same technique: here only the faces of the three girls have been allowed to develop normally.

● ABOVE A conventional print from a Polaroid camera back.

● RIGHT Before the print could develop, the backing sheet was separated and laid on wet paper. It was pressed into the paper with a rubber roller and left to develop. Peeling away the backing left this striking image.

● BELOW This still life was created in the same way, but a different textured paper was used.

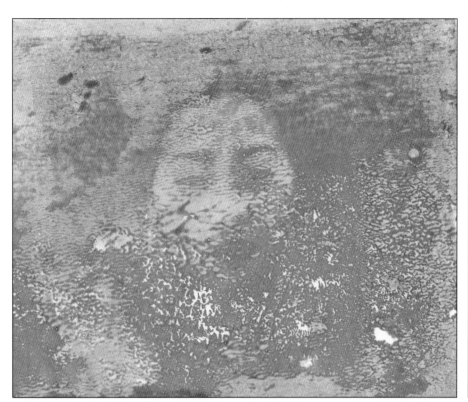

PERSPECTIVE

IMPROVING YOUR TECHNIQUE

In photography, perspective means creating a feeling of depth. There are several ways to get this effect and all of them are quite simple. It is strange, then, that so many photographs lack this element which can make all the difference to a shot.

In landscape photography the easiest way of gaining a sense of perspective is to use a foreground. Often you can add a tree at one side of the frame, or with its foliage filling the top of the picture.

This simple addition creates an illusion, the impression that there is space between the viewpoint, the foreground and the background. Compare this to a picture with no foreground features – it will look flat and dull.

Strong, naturally-formed lines can create a powerful sense of 'linear' perspective. Try standing at the end of a recently ploughed field. Look at the lines of the furrows running away from you. They will converge towards a

central point in the distance – what in the formal study of perspective is called a vanishing point. Taken from a low viewpoint these lines will create a strong feeling of depth.

When photographing buildings it is not difficult to exaggerate perspective. A shot of the front of a building taken straight on may lack impact whereas a more dramatic effect may be achieved by moving in close and looking up so the verticals converge.

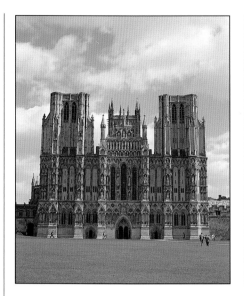

● ABOVE In this picture of Wells Cathedral the viewpoint was directly to the front. Although it shows all the façade it lacks depth. There is no sense of perspective at all.

● ABOVE Here the viewpoint is much closer. The camera is tilted upwards and the two towers converge towards the top centre of the frame. This creates a much more powerful image.

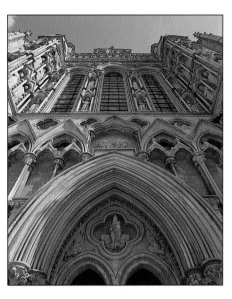

● ABOVE The viewpoint is nearer still and the verticals converge even more sharply. This slight change of viewpoint and camera angle greatly increases the perspective effect.

● ABOVE Another example of linear perspective: the bicycles create a seemingly endless line converging at an infinite distance. Lines of objects of any kind are one of the most effective ways of conveying perspective.

● RIGHT These red buses snaking down London's Oxford Street give a good sense of linear perspective. The uniformity of their colour adds to the feeling of depth.

● LEFT Placing this bale in the foreground and going quite close to it with a 21 mm wide angle lens creates a feeling of separation between it and the other bales, and the farm buildings beyond. This is a simple technique for adding perspective to your photographs.

MULTIPLE EXPOSURES

A camera with a facility for multiple exposures – that is, taking more than one picture on the same piece of film – allows unusual images and in the right hands can give stunning effects.

When planning a multiple image shot it is important to remember that light subjects will show up on dark areas. Try to frame the subjects so that a dark area is placed where a subsequent image will have a light subject, or vice versa. Images with large amounts of light areas are not suitable for multiple exposures. For instance, a great area of sky in one image will more or less obliterate anything else that appears in that part of the picture. As with any new technique, practice is necessary.

HOW TO USE VIEWFINDER SCREENS

A range of screens is available for many SLR cameras. A grid screen is best for multiple image shots. It is marked with a grid of vertical and horizontal lines which allows exact positioning of each image. The screen fits under the pentaprism on top of the camera. Release this, take out the existing screen, drop in the new one and put back the prism.

● BELOW At first glance this picture of the Palace of Holyroodhouse in Scotland may not look like a multiple image. But look at the sky. It is in fact a sequence of ten separate exposures taken at 30 second intervals. Each time the clouds were in a different position. By the final exposure they had moved a considerable way, giving the effect of a celestial explosion.

MULTIPLE EXPOSURES WITHOUT SPECIAL FACILITIES

This can be done on many ordinary SLR cameras. It needs some practice to get it right. To take three pictures on one frame, take the first picture in the normal way. Turn the film rewind crank as though rewinding the film back into the cassette, but *do not* press the rewind button. When the slack in the film has been taken up, then press the rewind button. Turn the rewind crank 1½ turns and release the rewind button. Take the next picture and repeat the process. Next take the third picture and then advance the film in the normal way.

● RIGHT This multiple exposure shot was taken indoors against a black background and lit by flash. First, the model was positioned at the left side of the frame, looking to the right. Then he was positioned looking the other way, and the camera was moved so that he was at the right of the frame. The result is a striking shot of both sides of his face in a single image.

● RIGHT The same technique was used in this picture, except that the first image was taken much closer in than the next two. This has made the central image much more dominant than the others. With such a technique care must be taken that the close-up image does not come out distorted.

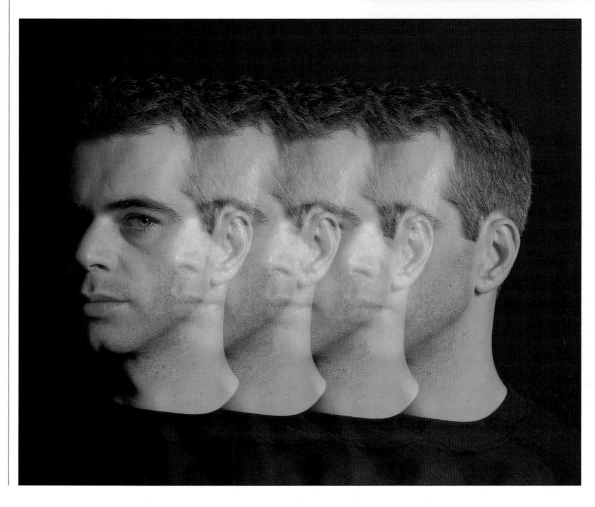

● LEFT In this sequence of four exposures the camera was moved slightly sideways after each exposure. It is important to avoid making multiple exposure shots simply confusing.

SHOOTING AGAINST THE LIGHT

● BELOW In this picture the sun is at about 45 degrees behind the young girl. A reflector was used to bounce back a small amount of light into her face. Without this she would have been almost silhouetted against the background. Although a lens hood was used, flare can still be seen in the top left-hand corner of the picture.

Many people think that you can only take good photographs if the sun is directly behind or to one side of the camera. Admittedly, by taking shots straight into the sun, flare and incorrect exposure may result, but if handled carefully these can be avoided or used to dramatic effect. To eliminate flare, a good lens hood should suffice. In fact you should always have a lens hood attached to your camera whichever way you are shooting. Flare can result from light indirectly reflecting off a shiny surface such as a car or window as well as directly from the sun.

Calculating exposure needs careful consideration as, if your subject is strongly backlit, it could appear as a silhouette. Although this may be the effect you are after, an adjustment to exposure will be necessary if you want your subject to be visible. If you are using a camera with built-in metering that has a choice of exposure modes such as average, centre-weighted or spot metering, then the spot metering mode will give a more accurate reading. If your camera only has metering in the average exposure mode, the chances are that it will underexpose your subject.

It is possible to overcome this if you can move in close so that the viewfinder is covering only the subject and take your meter reading at this distance. This means depressing the shutter release button about half-way. If your camera has an autoexposure lock you now keep the shutter release button

● ABOVE By exposing for the light reflecting off the water behind this boy fishing, he is shown almost in silhouette. In this case it works well because it is still obvious what activity he is involved in and the quality of the sparkling light bouncing off the water adds a romantic feel.

● LEFT A combination of a long lens and small aperture have resulted in isolating this plant from its surroundings. The back light has helped to emphasize this effect and the eye is drawn immediately to its delicate blooms.

● LEFT Often there is no time to use fill-in flash or a reflector to throw light back onto a subject, and this is often the case with animals. By exposing for the shadows enough detail has been retained to record this cat's peaceful posture in the shade.

slightly depressed and return to your original viewpoint. Without taking your finger off the button take your shot. Your subject will now be correctly exposed although the background will be overexposed. If you are taking more than one shot from this viewpoint you will have to repeat the procedure with each shot.

Another way round this problem is to use the exposure compensation dial – if applicable – on your camera. Set the dial to give two stops more exposure than the reading on the camera meter. If you can operate your camera manually and you have a separate exposure meter then, as above, you could move in close to your subject to take a reading.

If you do use this method with your camera or a hand-held meter, care must be taken not to cast a shadow on your subject, otherwise an incorrect reading will be obtained and overexposure will result. The preferred method of taking a reading with a hand-held meter is to use the incident light method. This means attaching an invercone – a white disc – to the exposure meter sensor. The meter is then pointed to the camera and a reading taken. This method records the amount of light falling on your subject as opposed to reflecting from it.

One word of warning when taking photographs into the light: the sun is very powerful and can be greatly magnified by camera lenses, so if these are pointed to the sun damage to your eyes could result – be careful!

● BELOW By shooting straight into the sun a very dramatic backlit picture has been obtained. A lens hood is essential in a case like this to eliminate flare. Be careful when shooting into the sun that you do not point the camera directly towards it, to avoid damage to your eye.

THROUGH GLASS

There are many ways of changing the appearance of a subject. One of the easiest is to photograph through glass. This can create a whole range of fascinating images with a minimum of equipment. The technique can also be used to change the appearance of photographs taken previously, by copying them through glass.

Both plain and patterned glass can be used. Many patterns are on sale, and some of them produce interesting distortions or multiple images. Colour can be introduced by adding a 'gel' – a sheet of coloured acetate.

There are several techniques for photographing an object through glass. The object may be placed on the glass and backlit, perhaps with a gel under the glass. The object may be put under the glass; a sheet of plain glass can be

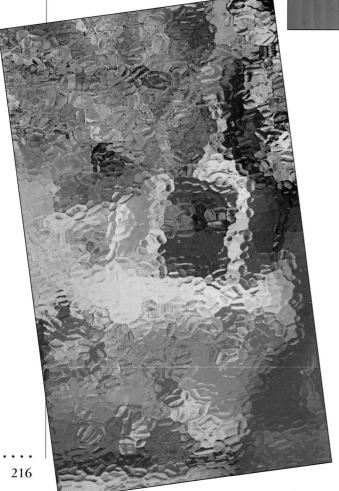

spattered with water to give the effect of looking through a window on a rainy day. An autofocus camera may not be able to decide whether to focus on the object or the glass. If the camera has a focus lock, mount it on a tripod, remove the sheet of glass, lock the focus on the object and replace the glass.

Such photographs are often taken from quite close in. A macro lens or extension rings or bellows will allow really close shots which can often give new effects.

When backlighting a subject, make sure that the front lighting is weaker, otherwise the backlight may not show up sufficiently.

As with any special technique, there is no limit to the effects that may be obtained by exercising a little imagination and being prepared to experiment.

● ABOVE This painting was photographed through glass and was lit by available light. The distance of the glass from the subject alters the final effect. The nearer the glass, the more defined the subject; the further away it is, the more obscure the image will seem.

● FAR LEFT This abstract image resembles a painter's palette and was created by placing brightly coloured objects under a sheet of glass.

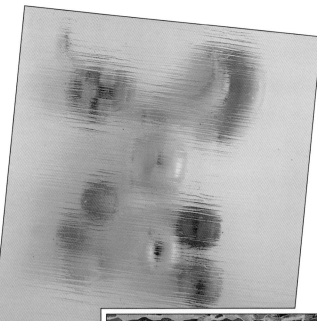

● LEFT Attractive still life images can be produced through glass. Here fruit is lit by available light using a reflector. Many different objects lend themselves to this concept; the effects can be seen immediately and can be altered as required.

● RIGHT By using a different pattern of glass over a painting another effect is achieved. Here the glass is placed further from the subject and the degree of obfuscation is increased.

ABSTRACT VIEWS

There are many ways of photographing everyday objects to give them a completely new and unfamiliar look. Sometimes the images may be so transformed that the picture becomes abstract or surreal. To achieve such an effect calls for an eye for composition and an understanding of how the image will appear on film, rather than how it looks to the eye.

One example is a moving object such as a flag fluttering in the breeze. To the eye it simply looks like a moving flag. It is not blurred, nor is it frozen into a particular momentary shape; however, if it is photographed it will appear in one of these ways. If a fairly slow shutter speed is used, and the moment is well judged so that the flag falls subtly into the frame, a strikingly dynamic image will result. A fast shutter speed could freeze the flag into a sharp image, but in comparison this will look stiff and lifeless.

This is only one example of seeing in an abstract way. Other images can be created by selecting part of an object, for example a building, which in isolation forms an abstract shape. Often the most ordinary objects or views can take on an abstract quality when viewed from a new angle.

There are no hard and fast rules as to what makes a good abstract picture. An acute eye will see the photographic potential in any scene.

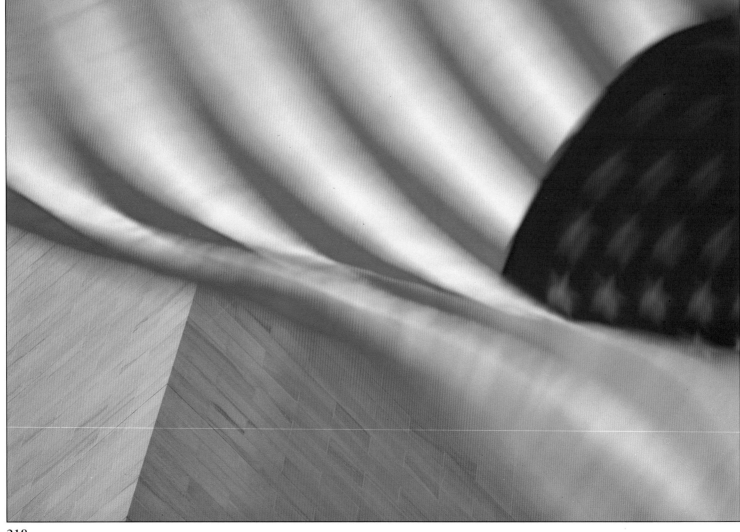

● LEFT Taken at dusk from a low viewpoint, the white gate stands out from its darker surroundings. The angle exaggerates the perspective and gives a strong lead into the picture. The slow shutter speed has allowed the tail-light of a passing car to leave a red streak. This dash of vivid colour adds a curious, almost surreal feel to the picture.

● BELOW LEFT The American flag was flying near the Washington Monument. The camera was angled upward so that part of the monument could be seen, forming a background and giving the one hard edge in the picture. The flag was moving gently in the wind. A series of pictures was taken at a shutter speed of ⅛ second. This created a swirling blur in the picture. Although it is abstract it expresses the movement of the flag in a way which a frozen image taken with a faster shutter speed could never have achieved.

● BELOW AND BOTTOM Both these pictures are sections of a building taken at slightly different angles and at different times of day. Both form abstract images, but the quality of light in each one has produced quite different results. There is an endless variety of ways of seeing an object. Re-examine familiar sights – there will always be a fresh way of looking at them.

DETAILS

Look at a magazine feature on travel at home or abroad. What strikes you about the photographs? More often than not, as well as the large scenic shots of landscapes and buildings there will be many smaller photographs. These may be used individually over several pages, or in a block on one page or double-page spread. Individually, any one of these little pictures may not make a great impression, but in their context all these small pictures unite to bring the photo documentary to life. They not only complement the big set pieces, they become important to the narrative as a whole.

The lesson to be learnt here is that wherever you are, you should be alert to the chance of getting these small but vital shots. Think of how they might fit into an album of your travels. You could even mount them as a collection in one frame. When you are taking the great view, the grand palace, look around at the immediate vicinity too. You will be surprised at what you find. All the pictures here were originally such 'secondary' shots, but they have all made it into various publications. One of them even became a magazine cover.

● BELOW The pattern of these woven African pots makes a pleasing picture in itself. Grouping them produces an interesting composition.

● RIGHT A detail of the ceiling of St Paul's Cathedral in London. In many churches the details of the decoration – mosaics, frescos, mouldings – are the most interesting thing. These can often be lost in one overall view of the interior.

● RIGHT This was taken while photographing the town of Sante Fé in New Mexico. It works as a composition because the vivid blue of the pot complements the terracotta of the wall. Both textures sit well together. As a vignette it would fit well into a mosaic of small shots of the town.

● ABOVE A sequence taken in a vineyard called not only for shots of the sweeping rows of vines but also for details of the grapes. They were shaded by the vine leaves, so a small reflector was used to bounce light back on to them. This has made them glow, so that they look even more succulent.

● LEFT Going in close to this locomotive wheel gives a strong geometrical pattern. The well-defined paintwork adds to the effect. Imagine this in a group with other details of the engine. It would make an interesting presentation of fine engineering.

COLLAGE

There are endless ways of making a photographic collage. The simplest can be made from a single image, which can be either a negative or a transparency. Alternatively, a highly complex design can be made from a large number of images.

To take the simplest case first, two prints could be made of a single image. Then the negative or transparency might be flipped over and another two prints made as a mirror image. The four prints could then be fitted together with a normal one the right way up at the top left, a mirror-image one the right way up at the top right, the other mirror image turned upside-down at bottom left, and the remaining normal one upside-down at bottom right. This will make a design with fourfold symmetry for a kaleidoscope effect. There are in fact four symmetrical ways of arranging these prints, and all could be tried to see which looks best. Such a collage could be enlarged endlessly by adding more prints to the outside, using the same image or a different one.

A more complicated design could be produced by cutting up the prints diagonally and fitting them together to make a radiating design. Again, more pieces of the same image or different one could be added in rings around the central circle.

Naturally there is no need to stick to a symmetrical design. A free-form collage can also give a stunning result.

● LEFT AND ABOVE Often the best kaleidoscopic collages are made with normal and reversed prints of a single image. This works particularly well with a landscape where there is strong detail on one side of the picture.

● BELOW Any image can be used to make a kaleidoscopic collage. The more detailed it is, the more complicated the final effect. These collages were made from a single photograph of a detail of the carving around the doorway of the cathedral in Orvieto, Italy. Even an image that is uninteresting in its own right can create a fascinating effect when treated in this way.

JOINER PICTURES

Joiner pictures were made famous by the artist David Hockney. They consist of a cluster of images joined together by quite literally sticking them to a board. Almost any subject lends itself to this treatment. All that is needed is imagination and a good eye for composition.

When making a joiner picture, it is important to remember that the aim is to create an imperfect join between images. They may be of different sizes or taken through different lenses. It is not even necessary for all the images to have been taken at the same session. A joiner could be made of shots taken outdoors of parts of the same scene over a period of hours. This would show different lighting and shadows as the sun moved across the sky.

Have the film processed at a laboratory which does borderless prints. Lay them out loosely at first and experiment with arrangements. Discard any prints that do not enhance the overall effect. When the design has crystallized, stick the prints down on a mounting board, bearing in mind that the picture will have irregular edges around which the board will be visible. A board that picks out one of the colours in the pictures might give the best effect.

Gradually-changing light is only one of the time effects that can be exploited in a joiner. For example, a city scene might show the changing traffic. The final image should show the viewer the scene as a series of different glances, much in the same way as it is seen by the eye in real life.

● BELOW This joiner picture of the River Thames and the Houses of Parliament in London was made from shots taken on colour print film. All the pictures were taken in a fairly short space of time, and all on the same film. Even so, variations in print density have occurred. Instead of being a distraction, these help to draw the eye to certain sections of the picture.

● RIGHT Building up joiner pictures enables the photographer to include the same person in different positions. In this picture the young boy appears on both sides of the shot and the photographer's feet can be seen in the bottom of the frame.

*S*ANDWICHING *T*RANSPARENCIES

Montages can be made not only with prints, but also by sandwiching together transparencies made with colour reversal film. A reasonable-sized collection of transparencies will probably yield quite a few pictures that would benefit from being combined.

Pictures discarded for being slightly overexposed are likely to be just the ones for this technique; so are correctly exposed pictures with plenty of highlights or a prevailing light tone. Do not try to put two dark subjects together: they will just absorb most of the light and the result will be muddy.

Skies, tree bark, water, leaves, even mud, can be used as an overlay for a more defined image such as a portrait, which should preferably be one taken against a white or pale background.

Try the combinations on a light box. When a good one is found, fix the two transparencies together with a narrow strip of clear tape wrapped around the blank edge of the film and put them in a plastic slide mount for projection or viewing. A really good image made by this method is worth having copied, though good copies of transparencies are quite expensive.

With some experience of sandwiching transparencies, it should be possible to see opportunities for shots which may not be too interesting on their own but will be ideal as part of a sandwich. These can be made into a collection for use when a suitable pair presents itself.

● LEFT The wheel of an army truck and a tree trunk form this sandwich.

● BELOW This girl was photographed against a white background. This image is combined with one of a dry river bed.

● LEFT Superimposing a portrait of a girl against a shot of a hedgerow has formed some interesting patterns.

● BELOW A girl's face is used against a photograph of a mushroom taken with a macro lens.

● BELOW LEFT One transparency was of a group of logs on end. The other was a section of a dry stone wall.

● BELOW RIGHT A combination of a girl's face photographed against a white background and part of a car window covered in raindrops produces this stylish image.

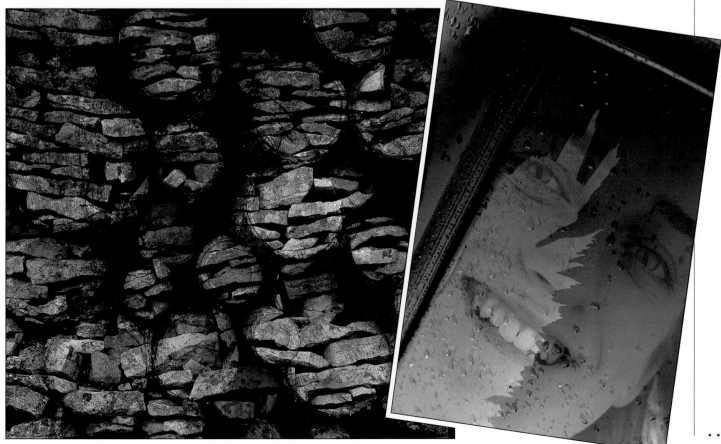

SHOOTING A STILL LIFE

Still life photography can be rewarding in more ways than just ending up with a pleasing image. Taking such pictures calls for patience and an eye for a good composition and theme. Still lifes are among the best of visual exercises. Innumerable famous painters, past and present, have turned to the still life at some time. Much of their work has in turn inspired photographers.

Almost any object can form part of a still life. There may be a collection of things with a particular link – for example, objects brought back from visits to a particular country. Such a collection could be interesting simply because everything came from that place. But everyday objects from home and around can be made into an equally satisfactory assemblage. When positioning the items, always check the view through the camera. When photographing flowers, which can wilt, or other fragile objects, add them to the arrangement last.

Equally, it is vital to pay attention to lighting. This conveys mood. A still life can be photographed in daylight, but shooting indoors gives far better control of lighting. There is no need for an elaborate studio or lots of lights; many pictures can be taken with a single light and a few reflectors and diffusers. A tiny adjustment of one of these, or of the position of an object, can make a great difference to the way a shadow falls and change the effect.

The shot will be taken from quite close in, probably using a standard lens or a medium telephoto. Every little detail will show up – a crease in a tablecloth, dust on a plate.

Undoubtedly the best camera to use for such work is a medium or large format one such as 5 × 4; but adequate results can be obtained on 35 mm if the composition is strong.

● LEFT Some of the best still life arrangements are the simplest. This one was constructed with a piece of rough marble. The two ceramic pieces are by the same potter. A drape of shiny cotton material completes the ensemble.

● LEFT The seashells and rocks were collected over some time, and photographed at home. They were laid on a slab of rough stone and the composition was arranged while constantly checking through the viewfinder. One light with a diffuser and two reflectors was used, and just before the shot was taken the whole area was lightly sprayed with water, using a fine houseplant mister.

● RIGHT This shot uses a black backdrop. A single light was placed above the pears, shining down on them from slightly behind. A large white reflector was placed in front of the camera, with a hole cut in it for the lens. A lens hood was used to keep stray light from falling on the lens itself. The reflector throws back a little light onto the pears so that they are softly illuminated.

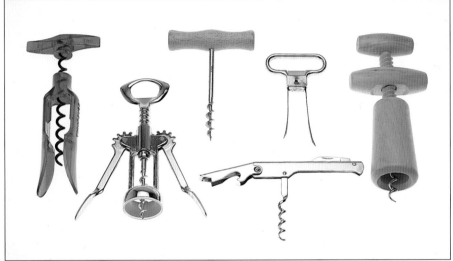

● LEFT Backlighting still life collections gives a very clean effect and can make the objects – in this case a collection of corkscrews – seem to float in space. They were laid on a piece of acrylic sheet lit from underneath, with another light directed down on them from above.

● LEFT These Mexican crafts objects had been collected over repeated visits to the country. A simple backdrop of rough timber was specially made. Two rugs were laid on a table and the assemblage built up, taking care that each item could be seen clearly. The two pictures were hung on the backdrop. A small light bulb was put in the lamp to create a realistic glow. The exposure time was 1 second to pick up this light; the rest of the picture was briefly lit by flash during this exposure.

FINDING PICTURES

There are many places where good pictures can be found, but it is easy to overlook them. Often they are camouflaged by their surroundings, or they need to be looked at from a different angle. Sometimes the chance of a picture appears suddenly, and if the camera is loaded and ready the opportunity can be seized.

When the picture is of a person, producing a camera may inhibit them and the chance of a great shot may be lost. But sometimes seeing the camera will make them strike a pose, and this may produce an image even better than the one that first caught the eye.

Simple and apparently uninspiring things can also be the basis of a great picture. It could be a wall, a fence or a door – perhaps the texture of peeling paint or weathered stone, or torn posters or graffiti.

To find these pictures what is chiefly required is constant awareness. There is usually no need for special or expensive equipment. Sometimes a picture is waiting to be taken, but this is not apparent from normal eye level. It may need a high or low viewpoint, or the different field of view given by a wide angle or telephoto lens to fit the composition into the frame.

Take time to evaluate the surroundings. Look at them selectively. With practice, even the most ordinary places and objects can be made to yield striking images that most people simply overlook. Even if the first attempts largely fail it is worth persevering. And even then, a collection of images that are not particularly interesting in themselves can often make a successful collage or series of pictures on a theme.

● RIGHT Looking for different angles can often result in original and unusual pictures. This one was taken while lying on the ground and looking upwards. The train couplings form a strong shape that seems to be a strange mechanical mating ritual. Always try a different viewpoint before giving up an idea as unpromising.

● ABOVE This picture came into view on a stroll down a street in New York City. The surface is the rear of a street vendor's stall. It is made of aluminium and has been rubbed down several times to remove graffiti. This has formed interesting patterns and some rather ominous shapes. The photograph of the girl is worn but her hopeful expression is still visible. Like the surface it is stuck to, the image is monochromatic, but the remains of another poster add a touch of red and blue. It is satisfying to think that over the months hundreds of thousands of people have passed this stall, but probably no one else has seen the chance of a picture.

● LEFT The original idea was to photograph the building, but while this was being done the man leaned out of the window with an enquiring look. He spoke no English, but a little sign language persuaded him to stay put while the lens was changed for a telephoto. He turned out to be a willing subject, and after a few shots suggested including his dog. The dog posed as uninhibitedly as he did. Without these two posturing figures the picture would have been dull, but by seizing a chance opportunity a good picture was obtained.

Pets

IMPROVING YOUR TECHNIQUE

Pets are always a favourite subject. Before you start to photograph them, it is most important to realize that although pets cannot speak they do have ways of communicating. If you endlessly try to get a dog to do something it does not want to do, it is never going to look happy and the shot will betray its mood. Eventually it will snap at you or even bite. You do have to take this seriously, especially if you are using pets and children together. Both get bored quickly, and when the session is no longer a game for them, stop.

So you will need to work quickly. An autofocus lens and TTL exposure control will be an asset. Very often it is the fleeting expression that makes the

shot. Going in close helps to capture this. A medium telephoto lens, say 100 mm, would be a good choice. This will help to fill the frame without getting too close to your subjects and disturbing them.

Try to avoid dressing animals up. The best shots are natural ones, not dogs wearing dresses or cats in sunglasses.

As well as shots for the album or framing, pictures of pets are ideal for Christmas and birthday cards.

Most animals grow faster than we do. Keep photographing them: taking a shot every month of your puppy or kitten will form an interesting record of its development.

● ABOVE LEFT Children with pets make very good subjects for photographs. But in both cases their attention soon wanders. When you see either tiring or becoming agitated it is time to stop.

● ABOVE RIGHT Some pets are more docile than others. This donkey in Ireland allowed plenty of time to move around and choose the best viewpoint. The background is blurred by using a wide aperture and fast shutter speed. The donkey's face is sharp and crisp, and the shot was taken just as it pricked up its ears.

● RIGHT The dog looks alert and the fishing net makes an interesting prop. Autofocus and TTL exposure metering help you to work quickly when photographing pets.

● LEFT, ABOVE AND BELOW These are ideal shots for a Christmas card. A simple prop such as the holly used here is all that was needed to set the scene. The backdrop is a graduated one shading from white to black, and the scene is lit by flash.

FIREWORKS

Photographs of fireworks are fun to take and good to look at. As with so many successful photographs, a little advance planning is necessary to ensure success. If photographing at a public display, get there early. It makes no difference what the weather is like: even in pouring rain people will flock to see a first-class display. Once in position, try to find out where the fireworks will go off.

Many of the most successful shots of fireworks, especially of rockets or other aerial displays, are in fact multiple exposures. There are two ways to achieve these shots. In either case the camera should be set on a tripod and a cable release fitted. Try to ensure that no one will jostle the camera – this can be difficult in a crowd. Point the camera at the place where the rockets are expected to explode.

If the camera has a multiple exposure device, take two or three shots of the rockets. For 100 ISO film the correct exposure is in the region of 2 seconds at f5.6.

If the camera will not take multiple exposures, set the aperture to the same size but turn the shutter ring to the B or T setting. Have a lens cap or some other device ready for covering the lens. Before the rockets go off, cover the lens and fire the shutter. If using the B setting, keep the cable release depressed. When the rockets explode, take off the cap for about 2 seconds, then replace it. Repeat this two or three times, then close the shutter by letting go of the cable release (for B) or pressing it again (for T).

● RIGHT AND TOP INSET These pictures were taken with multiple exposures – in each case, three pictures from the same position. The film was 100 ISO, and the aperture was f5.6. Each of the exposures was 2 seconds. It was raining, and a large lens hood was used to keep raindrops off the lens.

● ABOVE Photographs of individual fireworks
can be quite effective. Depending on the
brightness of the firework, an exposure of 2 to
4 seconds at f5.6 will probably be right.

● BELOW Flash can be used for firework shots to
light something else in the foreground, in this case
the boy. The exposure for this picture was 5
seconds at f8. The flash was set for f8, correctly
illuminating the boy, while the rest of the
exposure time recorded the trail of the sparkler.

The ancient Chinese proverb that 'a picture is worth a thousand words' has never been truer than it is today. Even with the rapid growth of on-the-spot television reporting, still images have a key role in conveying the intrinsic nature of a story. In modern history it is the still photograph taken in war, famine or natural disaster that stays in people's memory. On a lighter note, it is very often the photograph on the cover of a magazine that will persuade the consumer to buy it.

Photographs can tell a story in many different ways. The pictures here may not make up what many people would think of as a story, but they tell us quickly what this man is associated with: ancient music and instruments. On the shoot many pictures were taken of him in his workshop, cutting, chiselling, glueing, polishing, tuning. Further shots showed the craftsman by himself, with his instruments, in his home. And many were taken of the instruments themselves. When it came to editing all these it was decided that a strong portrait with one of his instruments was required. Another decision was to show the detail of many finished instruments, rather than have a story of the making of a single one. Different angles showed the elegant curves of the lutes' bodies. The detail in the frets and roses showed the delicacy of the craftsmanship. Keeping the lighting low emphasized the featured part of each instrument. Restricting the picture sequence to these shots has let the feeling of precision, sensitivity and sheer art shine through.

When you are planning to photograph a person or their work, or an event, try to see how several shots can be used. You may be photographing a member of your family for the album rather than shooting a sequence for a magazine, but think of how you can create a series of shots that will make an attractive and rewarding layout. It may seem difficult to edit your pictures – even wasteful – but to do justice to your best shots good presentation is vital, and so a wide selection is important.

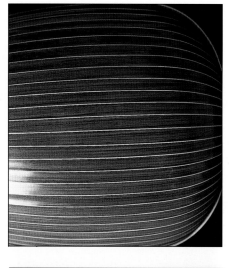

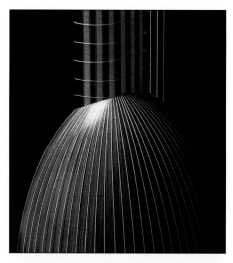

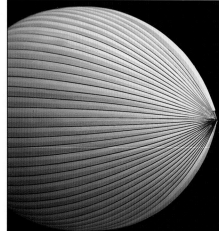

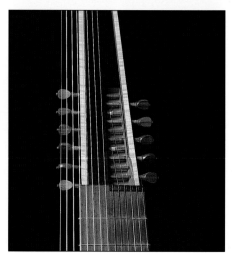

● A sequence of close-up, detailed shots portrays the subject matter, while a larger portrait of the craftsman himself neatly completes the picture story.

In a world where colour photography has become the norm people are often surprised at the power of the images produced by black and white. This is particularly the case where a serious subject or a sombre mood has to be portrayed. Black and white can convey squalor and misery in a way that colour can never do. The memorable images of great documentary photographers such as Don McCullin remain in the mind partly because they are shot in stark black and white.

When telling a story in black and white, the basic ingredients are much as they would be for a colour sequence, but the vital things to look for are tone and texture.

Make a plan of the kind of pictures that are needed before starting to shoot. Look at photo features in a news magazine. The number of pictures used in one story is usually quite small, and each one has a purpose. If the geographical location of the story is relevant, there must be a picture that gives the viewer some idea of what the place looks like.

If the story is one based on people, try to get to know them first. Not only will they supply information, they will take more kindly to a photographer who is interested in them and who seems to be including them in his work, rather than snapping them surreptitiously from behind a tree. People in some regions, or in inner cities, may seem intimidating, but it is better to have them on one's side than to treat them as strangers, which only invites hostility.

Medium speed film, about 400 ISO, is adequate for most situations. If necessary it can be uprated to a higher speed and also given a longer development time.

● LEFT Only by going in really close could this portrait be made to work. This man's leathery skin and tousled hair show what it means to live rough. He gladly accepted a cigarette and talked ramblingly, but sadly he seemed oblivious to what was going on around him.

● BELOW This picture tells us about the location: part of London's East End. The scruffy appearance gives us an indication of the surroundings. Little touches such as the cat sitting on a pile of rubbish add interest to an otherwise bleak scene.

● RIGHT Alcohol can be a refuge for many people, mainly men drinking openly on the streets, in doorways and in the few open spaces. Confronting such people may seem daunting, but sharing the time of day and a cigarette is less likely to arouse suspicion and ill-feeling than lurking behind a wall.

● ABOVE Nobody knew where this woman lived. She would appear nearly every morning at six when the café opened. She always had two cups of tea and a sandwich. She never said a word, but indicated that she did not mind having her picture taken. The viewpoint from one end of the table gives a strong sense of perspective. Many social statements could be read into the surroundings.

● LEFT This shot was taken near a street market. In one section people sell what others have long since discarded. This trader selling just a handful of items stands against a crumbling backdrop. It is a cold day and although he is well wrapped up, he still seems to be clutching himself to keep warm.

• A shot taken on black and white film and printed in the normal way.

PROCESSING TRICKS

Many areas of photography lend themselves to manipulation. Often such treatment goes completely against what is accepted as normal procedure; it might even be seen as a 'mistake'. Yet the results can be so exciting and dynamic that such mistreatment becomes a valid technique in its own right. Many such techniques do not need any special equipment or even a darkroom: just a camera and film.

For example, colour reversal film, which produces colour transparencies, is processed using a chemical solution known as E6. Colour negative film, which produces prints, is processed using C41. What happens if reversal film is processed using C41 or negative film is processed using E6? The colours go crazy in a completely unexpected way. Some films turn magenta, others bluish green. Start with one type of film and see what happens. Study carefully what has happened to each colour. This may give a pointer to more interesting results. Does the film need more exposure – for example, should 400 ISO film be rated at 100 ISO? Should it also be 'push processed' – given more development time than usual? Only persistence and careful evaluation of the results will give the answer. In any case, the technique will give wild results and these might include some great shots.

Another 'deliberate mistake' is to have black and white negatives printed on a colour printing machine. When a colour negative is printed the light passes through three filters: magenta, cyan and yellow. Asking the printer to print with only one of these filters will give a positive print in that colour. Try each filter in turn, or try two of them – for example, magenta and yellow combine to make red. Of course, a sympathetic processing lab is needed.

• The black and white negative printed on a colour machine, using only the yellow filter.

• The same negative printed through a magenta filter.

• Here the cyan filter was used.

• There are endless variations. This picture was printed through all three filters.

● ABOVE Here 100 ISO colour negative film was rated at 25 ISO and given the E6 process normally used for colour reversal film. The skin tones are quite bleached out, and the effect is much less vibrant.

● RIGHT This picture was taken on 64 ISO colour reversal film rated at 12 ISO and push processed half a stop in the C41 chemicals designed for use on colour negative film. This has increased the contrast and intensified the colour, especially on the floor and the yellow wall. A different type of film would have produced a totally different effect. Only trial and error will perfect the technique.

PHOTOCOPYING

• BELOW The addition of a hand-drawn border around a favourite photograph gives an extra quality to the final image. This border was photocopied and then cut out to accommodate the print. Slightly overlaying the border onto the photograph before re-photocopying it gives the effect of a single image.

One of the simplest yet most effective ways of producing prints from transparencies, photographic prints or 'video still' disk is a photocopying machine. Most large towns now have a photocopying centre with a variety of machines which will produce same-size copies, enlargements or reductions. The prints can be selectively enlarged and the colours manipulated. Sections of prints can be cut up and rearranged to form an instant collage.

As well as making prints onto paper, photocopied images can be transferred onto fabric; many shops offer a T-shirt printing service, for example, and liquid transfer kits are now available so that fabric can be decorated at home using colour photocopies.

Some photocopies produce prints directly from 35 mm transparencies by means of a projector. Positive prints can be produced from negatives, and vice versa. Colours can be greatly manipulated and images can be created by 'dragging'; this is where the original image is moved while the machine is in the process of scanning. Pictures can be

repeated and built up into a mosaic. Details such as jewellery or a hand, for instance, can be scanned individually and used as images on their own or overlaid with other details. By making a copy of a copy, the original image can be broken down to create an abstract graphic picture. Images can be printed using just a single colour or reproduced in black and white.

The obvious attraction of using a photocopier to produce a collage is that the effect can be seen immediately and adjustments can be made at once without having to wait for the film to be developed. Photocopying is an economical way to print favourite pictures as postcards or greetings cards, or for making a large mural that would be prohibitively expensive if produced using traditional photographic processes. The quality of this form of printing cannot be compared to a proper photographic enlargement but the scope for producing a variety of eye-catching images is endless.

• ABOVE By photocopying two different photographs, interesting collages can be made. The people from one picture were cut out and pasted onto a photocopy of another image. This in turn was re-photocopied. This simple technique means that family and friends can be transported to a totally different environment or country.

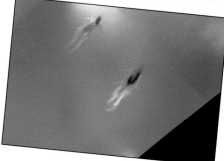

• RIGHT The most surreal results can be achieved by photocopying your holiday photographs. These two photographs, ABOVE, are not particularly interesting by themselves, but when placed together and photocopied the effect is visually intriguing. There appear to be two viewpoints: one of the swimmers under the water, and another from a higher viewpoint looking down on the pool.

• FAR LEFT The original black and white photograph was selectively hand-coloured using fluorescent inks. This was then photocopied; the result is a brightly coloured boat sailing on a monochromatic sea.

IMPROVING YOUR TECHNIQUE

● BELOW This picture was originally taken on 35 mm transparency film and then copied onto disk. The print was made using a thermal printer.

One of the newest innovations in photography is the video still camera. Unlike conventional cameras, the video still records an image on a small floppy disk, exactly like those used in personal computers. Each disk has the capacity to record up to 50 separate photographs. Instead of sending the disk away to be processed, as would be the case with 35 mm film, the images can be played back instantly on a television screen or computer monitor. They can also be recorded on video tape or run out as prints at the majority of photocopying stores, yet the pictures may not be as good as conventional images.

The video still camera itself looks and is operated in much the same way as a compact camera. It comes with a standard lens but has wide angle and telephoto attachments. It has built-in flash and a tripod adaptor. The

exposure selection is automatic and the focus is fixed, but there is a macro facility. Single, multi and self-timer shooting modes, back light control and a rechargeable battery are all standard; it is also a very quiet camera to operate. The conventional rechargeable battery is powerful enough to take 50 shots. An additional power pack is available that will enable you to take 4000 shots. The camera can also be worked directly from the mains as a true 'electronic' camera. There is a time lapse facility which allows a picture to be taken at various intervals, for instance either every minute or up to once every hour.

By using a video controller, the shots can be displayed and previewed backwards and forwards. The viewing sequence can be altered to meet different requirements and recorded on video tape for a permanent display.

● BELOW LEFT By looking at the recorded image on a computer screen, selected parts of a picture can be printed in much the same way as a conventional enlargement. This is a detail of a much larger photograph.

ADVANTAGES OF THE VIDEO STILL CAMERA

- Disks can be stored, edited or used repeatedly.

- The image is stored electronically so there is no need for lengthy conventional processing.

- Unlike conventional film, the disk cannot be 'fogged' and can be exposed to light without incurring any damage.

- Images recorded on disk are instantly ready for viewing just as on video tape.

- A range of accessories, including lenses, are readily available.

● ABOVE This strong image originated from a picture taken on a video still camera of a reflection in a shop window. The camera is at its best when shooting close in, but the scope for abstraction when put into the computer is where your creativity can excel.

● LEFT This full-length portrait was shot using available light filtering through an open window; it was recorded on a floppy disk and printed on a computer thermal printer.

● BELOW Colours can be altered or black and white prints made using a video still camera. This almost monochromatic picture was achieved by manipulating the original disk image in a computer. The scope for different variations and experiments from a single image is endless.

ENTERING COMPETITIONS

With growing skill, better equipment and more adventurous photography, it may be time to think of entering some pictures in competitions. There is nothing so encouraging as seeing your own work in print, in a magazine or a newspaper, or simply on display as a prizewinner.

Whatever the medium, there will be hundreds of entries – thousands in a national competition. The judges will be looking for technical excellence and originality of composition, but in the first place they will be looking for an image which exactly fits the theme set for that category. It is amazing how many entrants send in landscapes when the organizers have quite clearly stated that the subject was to be a building or a portrait.

Read the rules carefully. Only a single entry may be allowed in any one category. Prints should be clearly marked on the back with a name, address and telephone number. Sometimes these should be written on the entry form and this should be stuck to the print.

If a photograph really is good enough to enter, it is probably good enough to be made into a professional enlargement. This does not have to be huge; in fact most competitions stipulate a maximum and minimum print size. Discuss the proposed enlargement with the printer. Often a picture can be greatly enhanced if it is cropped, and perhaps angled slightly. Certain areas may benefit from being printed up or shaded.

When entering transparencies it is equally important to read the rules.

There is no point submitting a transparency in a beautiful professional black mask if the organizers want 35 mm slides for projection.

An appropriate caption is vital. A picture may be worth a thousand words, but if it comes to a tiebreak, a single witty or appropriate word can swing the result.

Finally, package entries carefully. A surprising number of pictures arrive creased or bent because they were not properly packed. Often such prints are discarded and not judged.

● LEFT This picture of a cemetery in northern France dedicated to the dead of the First World War has the makings of a worthy competition entry. It is correctly exposed throughout. The clouds in the blue sky are clearly defined. The lines of headstones form a strong composition complemented by the row of trees on the horizon.

● ABOVE Sometimes a shot taken some time ago suddenly fills the brief of a competition perfectly. This graphic image of an imminent storm could fit several competition categories. It was taken just before the sun was masked by clouds. The buildings are caught in a shaft of sunlight which isolates them from their gloomy surroundings.

● RIGHT A competition entry for a picture story or photo documentary is likely to include a character shot of a person. Look for a picture that says the most about the person and their surroundings, taken from an angle that makes the strongest composition.

● LEFT When entering black and white photographs make sure that the print is of the highest quality. Even the best exposed negatives can be further enhanced in the darkroom. Often the winning entry is the simplest of images beautifully printed and presented.

COULD YOU SELL YOUR PICTURES?

If pictures are good enough to enter in competitions they might also be good enough to sell. The right image in the right place and at the right time can sell an idea or product, or stimulate people's interests. Such a picture can be worth a lot of money.

Unlike many products, a picture – or rather, its reproduction rights – can be sold again and again. A single sale may bring in only a modest sum, but repeated sales over several years can notch up a tidy amount.

There are no rules about what makes a picture sell. Often an original and beautiful shot will sit in a drawer for ever because it does not fit into any particular subject area. However, one thing is for sure: a picture that is under- or overexposed, or out of focus, or simply badly composed, will not sell – no matter how interesting its subject may be.

For colour photographs, transparencies are preferred to negatives.

If a picture prominently features a person, a model release form from that person is a necessity. For groups of individuals, there must be a release form from each of them. Agencies will not consider publishing such pictures without the form.

Pictures can be submitted to a photo library, which will assure them wide coverage. A certain amount of trust is required from both parties when entering into such an arrangement. Only apply to a large and well-known library, which will be honest about how many times a picture has been used. It is worth asking other photographers or looking at the picture acknowledgements in books, newspapers and magazines to find out the names of reputable libraries.

● RIGHT These commuters are blurred but they convey the urgent movement of rush hour in a city. Such pictures have editorial and advertising uses. This one has been published many times in magazines and newspapers.

● LEFT This picture of London's famous department store, Harrods, has been published in one form or another all over the world, and has been used literally hundreds of times. Its most important ingredient is that it is instantly recognizable. It is also a good composition and correctly exposed.

● BELOW Good landscape pictures are always needed by local and national travel agencies, and magazines and newspapers running features on a country or region. Good composition, spot-on exposure, well-defined clouds and a strong, immediate point of interest are all vital ingredients in ensuring good and lasting sales.

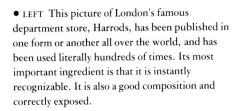

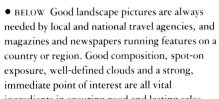

STOCKISTS AND SUPPLIERS

HEAD OFFICES
Advice on stockists and repairs

UK

Canon UK Ltd
Units 4, 5 & 6
Brent Trading Centre
North Circular Road
London NW10 0JF

Minolta (UK) Ltd
1–3 Tanners Drive
Blakelands North
Milton Keynes MK14 5BU

Nikon UK Ltd
Nikon House
380 Richmond Road
Kingston
Surrey KT2 5PR

USA

Canon USA Inc
1 Canon Plaza
Lake Success
NY 11042

Canon USA Inc
100 Park Boulevard
Itasca
IL 60143-2693

Canon USA Inc
5825 Oakbrook Parkway
Norcross
GA 30093

Canon USA Inc
123 Paularino Avenue East
Costa Mesa
CA 95054

Canon USA Inc
4000 Burton Drive
Santa Clara
CA 95054

Canon USA Inc
3200 Regent Boulevard
Irving
Texas 75063

Canon USA Inc
1020 Auahi Street
Building 8
Honolulu
Hawaii 96814

Canon USA Inc
5701 General Washington Drive
Alexandria
VA 22312

Minolta Corporation
101 Williams Drive
Ramsey
NJ 07446

Minolta Corporation
11150 Hope Street
Cypress
CA 90630

Minolta Corporation
3000 Tallview Drive
Rolling Meadows
IL 60008

Nikon Inc
1300 Walt Whitman Road
Melville
NY 11747-3064

Nikon Inc
19601 Hamilton Avenue
Torrance
CA 90502-1309

Nikon Inc
5355 Oakbrook Parkway
Norcross
GA 30093

CANADA

Canon Canada Inc
6390 Dixie Road
Mississauga
Ontario L5T 1P7

Canon Canada Inc
10652 Côte de Liesse
Lachine
Quebec H8T 1A5

Canon Canada Inc
2828 16th Street
NE Calgary
Alberta T2E 7KY

Minolta Canada Inc
369 Britannia Road East
Mississauga
Ontario 14Z 2H5

Minolta Canada Inc
3405 Thimens Boulevard
St Laurent
Quebec H4R 1V5

Minolta Canada Inc
105–3830 Jacombs Road
Richmond
BC V6V 1Y6

Nikon Canada Inc
1366 Aerowood Drive
Mississauga
Ontario L4W 1C1

Nikon Canada Inc
No 5 13511 Crestwood Place
Richmond
BC V6V 2E9

Nikon Canada Inc
3300 Chemin Côte Vertu
Montreal
Quebec H4R 2B7

AUSTRALIA

Canon Australia Pty Ltd
1 Thomas Holt Drive
North Ryde
NSW 2113

NEW ZEALAND

Canon Optics New Zealand Ltd
Fred Thomas Drive
Takapuna
PO Box 33–336
Auckland

SPECIALIST DEALERS

UK

Fox Talbot Cameras
443 Strand
London WC2R 0QU

Keith Johnson & Pellings
93–103 Drummond Street
London NW1 2HJ

Keith Johnson & Pellings
Unit 8
Barclay Hill Place
Portlethen Industrial Estate
Aberdeen AB1 4PF

Keith Johnson & Pellings
Unit 7
Montpelier Central Station Road
Montpelier
Bristol BS6 5EE

Keith Johnson & Pellings
Unit 3
Loughside Industrial Park
Dargan Crescent
Duncrue Road
Belfast BT3 9JP

Leeds Photovisual Ltd
20–26 Brunswick Centre
Bernard Street
London WC1N 1AE

Leeds Photovisual Ltd
Charlton Place
Downing Street
Manchester M12 6HH

Leeds Photovisual Ltd
2 Newhall Place
16–17 Newhall Hill
Hockley
Birmingham B1 3JH

Leeds Photovisual Ltd
Lovell House
North Street
Leeds LS2 7PN

Leeds Photovisual Ltd
30–30A Lee Way
Lee Way Industrial Estate
Newport
Gwent NP9 0TW

The Studio Workshop
153 Farringdon Road
London EC1R 3AD

USA

Sinar Bron Inc
17 Progress Street
Edison
NJ 08820

CANADA

Lisle-Kelco Ltd
3525 Nashua Drive
Mississauga
Ontario L4V 1R1

AUSTRALIA

Baltronics
Unit 8
Chuter Place
Holt Street
North Sydney
NSW 2060

NEW ZEALAND

CR Kennedy (NZ) Ltd
PO Box 14-058
Panmure
Auckland

SOUTH AFRICA

Photra Photo
PO Box 9072
Johannesburg 2000

GLOSSARY

ASA
American Standards Association: a series of numbers that denote the speed of a film; now superseded by the ISO number.

APERTURE
Opening at the front of the camera that determines the amount of light passing through the lens to the film.

APERTURE PRIORITY
A metering system in the camera that allows the photographer to choose the aperture while the camera selects the shutter speed.

B SETTING
Indication on shutter speed dial that allows the shutter to remain open for as long as the shutter release is depressed.

BARN DOORS
Attachment that fits on the front of a studio light and allows the photographer to control the spread of light.

BETWEEN-THE-LENS SHUTTER
Usually built in to a lens, this type of shutter allows flash synchronization at any shutter speed.

BRACKETING
Method of exposing one or more exposures on either side of the predicted exposure to obtain the best result.

CDS
Cadmium sulphide cell; used in electronic exposure meters.

CABLE RELEASE
Cable which allows the shutter to be fired with minimum vibration or camera shake; essential for long exposures.

CAMERA MOVEMENTS
Found on large format cameras, these allow the photographer to move the front and back panels of the camera.

CASSETTE
Light-tight container for holding 35 mm film.

COLOUR NEGATIVE FILM
Film that produces negatives for prints.

COLOUR REVERSAL FILM
Film that produces transparencies or slides.

COLOUR TEMPERATURE
A scale for measuring the quality of light in values of kelvin.

CONTACT SHEET
Method for printing negatives the same size as the film so that the photographer can choose the images to be enlarged.

CYAN
Blue-green light; the complementary colour to red.

DIN
Deutsche Industrie Norm; German method of numbering the speed of a film now superseded by ISO numbering.

DX CODE
Bar code on a 35 mm cassette that contains information such as film speed. This is read inside the camera which adjusts itself automatically.

DARK SLIDE
Container for holding a sheet of film; used in large format cameras.

DAYLIGHT-BALANCED COLOUR FILM
Colour film that is balanced for use in daylight light sources at 5400 kelvin.

DEPTH OF FIELD
The distance in front of the point of focus and the distance beyond that is acceptably sharp.

DIAPHRAGM
The adjustable aperture of a lens.

DIFFUSER
Material placed in front of the light source that softens the quality of the light.

EXPOSURE METER
Instrument for measuring the amount of light available that can be read to indicate shutter speed and aperture.

EXTENSION BELLOWS
Extendable device that fits between the lens and the camera body that enables the photographer to take close-up shots with a variable degree of magnification.

EXTENSION TUBES
Tubular device that fits between the lens and the camera body to enable the photographer to take close-up pictures. The degree of close-up available varies with the length of the tube used.

F NUMBER
A scale of numbers that indicate the size of the aperture used i.e. f2.8, f4, f5.6, f8, f11, f16 etc. Sometimes referred to as stops.

FILTERS
Coloured glass, plastic or gelatin that alters the colour of the light falling on the film when placed over the lens.

FIXED FOCUS
Camera that has no means of altering the focus of the lens; usually only found on the cheapest cameras.

FOCAL PLANE SHUTTER
Shutter method that exposes the film to light by using a moving blind in the camera body.

HIGH KEY
Photography where most of the tones are from the light end of the scale.

HOT SHOE
Electrical contact usually found on the top of 35 mm SLR cameras; forms part of the camera's flash synchronization.

ISO
International Standards Organization: the numbering system now used to indicate the speed of a film.

INCIDENT LIGHT READING
Method of taking an exposure meter reading by recording the amount of light falling on the subject.

LIGHT BOX
An illuminated box used for viewing transparencies or negatives.

LOW KEY
Photography where most of the tones are from the dark end of the scale.

MACRO LENS
Lens that enables the photographer to take close-up pictures without the need for extension tubes or bellows.

MAGENTA
Blue-red light. The complementary colour to green.

MONTAGE
Picture made up of a collection of other images.

PANNING
Method of moving the camera in line with a moving subject such as a racing car. This produces a blurred background but keeps the subject sharp, thereby giving a greater effect of movement in the final image.

PARALLAX
The difference between what the camera viewfinder sees and what the lens sees. This difference is eliminated in SLR cameras.

PERSPECTIVE CONTROL (PC) LENS
Lens that can be adjusted at right angles to its axis. This enables the photographer to alter the field of view without moving the camera. Also known as a shift lens.

POLARIZING FILTER
Filter that enables the photographer to darken blue skies and cut out unwanted reflections.

RANGEFINDER CAMERA
System that allows sharp focusing on a subject by aligning two images in the camera viewfinder.

RECIPROCITY FAILURE
Situations where shots requiring exposures of longer than 1 second result in a loss of film speed; this leads to underexposure.

SLR
Single lens reflex; type of camera that allows the photographer to view the subject through the actual lens, via a mirror that moves out of the way when the picture is taken.

SHIFT LENS
Alternative name for perspective control lens.

SHUTTER
Means of controlling the amount of time light is allowed to pass through the lens onto the film.

STOP
Also known as the f number.

T SETTING
Indication on shutter speed dial that allows the shutter to remain open when the shutter release is depressed and close when it is depressed again.

TTL
Camera that assesses the exposure required by taking a reading through the camera lens.

TUNGSTEN-BALANCED COLOUR FILM
Colour film that is balanced for use in artificial light sources at 3400 kelvin.

ZOOM LENS
Lens with variable focal length.